Lambeth:

A View from the Two Thirds World

LAMBETH:

A View from the
Two Thirds World

Vinay Samuel
and Christopher Sugden

First published in Great Britain 1989

SPCK
Holy Trinity Church
Marylebone Road
London NW1 4DU

British Library Cataloguing in Publication Data

Samuel, Vinay Kumar
  Lambeth: a view from the two-thirds
  world.
  1. Developing countries. Christian church
  I. Title   II. Sugden, Chris
  270

  ISBN 0–281–04420–1 (net edition)
  ISBN 0–281–04443–0 (non-net edition for Africa,
  Asia, S. Pacific and Caribbean)

Typeset by Latimer Trend & Company Ltd, Plymouth
Printed in Great Britain by
Courier International Ltd, Tiptree, Essex

Contents

Introduction

At the close of the final service of the Lambeth Conference, the bishops filed out of Canterbury Cathedral towards their coaches for the journey back to the University of Kent. They greeted those whom they had got to know over the past three weeks. As the Bishop of Seoul passed us in the close, he gave us a small enamel brooch as a gift—it said 'Seoul Olympics 1988'.

The year 1988 was both a Lambeth year and an Olympic year, two highlights of international co-operation and encounter. If both events continue on their current schedule, they will not coincide again till the year 2028. The Olympics at Seoul were the first since 1976 not to suffer a boycott. The Lambeth Conference welcomed for the first time for forty years bishops from India, Pakistan, Burma and China, and double the number of African bishops as in 1978. In the conference room of the headquarters of the Church of the Province of Kenya is a black and white photograph of the 1968 Lambeth Conference, taken outside Lambeth Palace. Black faces are few and far between. In contrast, the photograph of the 1988 Conference is in colour, and out of over 600 faces, some 225 are coloured other than white.

This book is neither an alternative report of Lambeth '88, nor a record of the Conference by bishops from the Two Thirds World (a term preferred by residents of those parts of the world dominated by poverty, powerlessness, and religious pluralism, to the term 'Third World'). It is not a chronicle of the contributions of such bishops to Lambeth, though some are included. It offers a perspective on the Anglican Communion as it appeared at Lambeth '88.

The Lambeth Conference does not stand on its own. It does not even stand in strict relationship to previous Lambeth Conferences, as though one Conference must be understood primarily in relation to its predecessors. The Lambeth Conference is the most comprehensive and perhaps most comprehensible expression of the global Anglican Communion. For in its membership and meetings, its strengths and weaknesses, its unity and diversity, it dramatically pictures the nature of the communion. It provides a once-in-ten-years opportunity to survey the life of the communion in its totality, as given through the experiences and opinions of its global order of senior leaders, its diocesan bishops. The Conference must be understood in relation to that communion and to the world the communion is set in. We are using the occasion when all the diocesan bishops are gathered for three weeks together as the event which gives us clues as to what the Anglican Communion is, and what the composition of the communion with its dynamic growth in the Two Thirds World is all about.

This book attempts to examine the Lambeth Conference as an expression of that communion, and to analyse in particular what the presence of so many bishops from the Two Thirds World signified, represented and expressed. The pastoral letters and the reports of the four sections were published well after the Conference ended. This book does not attempt to cover the same ground, or even to review this material. It does seek to show how people from the Two Thirds World read it, and how we perceived others reading and interpreting such material.

Its authors are not bishops. But we were privileged to be companions to many of the bishops during the Conference. Some we took out for meals, others we took shopping. We even escorted one archbishop for a haircut—to the delight of his wife. For some we were chauffeurs, for others we made travel and visa arrangements. Many we got to know as friends. We listened to every debate in the plenary sessions from a bird's eye vantage point in the press gallery, and we asked questions in every press conference. For the greater part of each day, we sat with bishops in the coffee lounges and their own rooms. We interviewed them about their perspectives on the Conference in conversations of between half an hour and an hour's length; these we taped with their permission and have had transcribed. We are most grateful to the seventy-five bishops, archbishops, presiding bishops, bishops' wives, consultants, members of the Anglican Consultative Council and its staff from every continent who spared us time out of their punishing schedules. We are also grateful to the twenty bishops, including the Archbishop of Canterbury, who, after Lambeth, took time to complete our informal questionnaire on their perspectives on the Conference.

This book does not give a blow by blow description of the programme of the Conference. Instead, it describes the Conference in terms of its significance for the Two Thirds World bishops. What was important for *them*?

CHAPTER 1

Guests of the Archbishop

In 1978 there were 80 bishops from Africa at the Lambeth Conference; 175 came in 1988. We know of two dioceses in Africa which are due to divide within two or three years. If such trends continue, over 300 African bishops will be at the 1998 Lambeth Conference. As Bishop David Gitari of Mount Kenya East told us, 'Anyone who wants a resolution passed in 1998 will have to come to terms with the African Bishops.'

From presence to perspectives

It is not enough to note with satisfaction the strength of the representation from Africa at Lambeth '88. We must examine the phenomenon of the colourful presence of so many non-white people from the Two Thirds World and ask what it meant; how they understand themselves as members of the Anglican Communion; how they understand their episcopal role in their own situations, what perspectives they brought to the Conference and how they understood and related to the Conference itself and its decision-making processes.

As we shall see, bishops from the Two Thirds World changed the content and agenda of the Conference during the Conference itself. They were the significant force in the debates on evangelism and culture, polygamy, other faiths, and homosexuality; they brought the largest number of resolutions to the Conference plenary sessions. Significantly, the Conference handed much greater responsibility in the communion to the 27 primates, of whom 18 are from the Two Thirds World.[1] To understand their role in the 1988 Lambeth Conference, and for anyone preparing for the 1998 Lambeth, it would be wise to know what terms the African bishops and their Two Thirds World colleagues set and are likely to set for the Anglican Communion. What is the meaning of Anglicanism for them?

St Paul's and the Palace—the Raj revisited?

On the second Tuesday of the Conference, just halfway through, bishops and their wives got up early on a lovely day to board 28 coaches to London at 7 a.m.(British Rail had double booked their excursion train that day). They arrived at the steps of St Paul's Cathedral about half an hour early. City yuppies in the heart of the financial capital of what had been the world's largest empire were treated to the sight of hundreds of figures in purple plumage and their wives milling round on the steps of their city's cathedral.

We had rubbed shoulders for ten days with a cynical British media in the press building at Canterbury. Some of its cynicism may have rubbed off on us for, in the half-hour that it took for the bishops to process from the burial place of Wellington and Nelson to take their places under Christopher Wren's dome, we found ourselves asking whether this was the religious hangover of Empire, fossilized in the religious structure that had endorsed it.

We wondered if the British Empire was still alive in this procession of those who had grown up after the sun had set. For it seemed as if the Archbishop of Canterbury, as he walked at the end of the procession with the primates, was the benign white father with his prefects, presiding over a school service for the nicely turned-out boys from mission schools, looking like 500 choirboys (as Bishop John Walker, the black bishop of Washington, USA, thinks of their robes) in their scarlet and white with ruffs at their wrists. And had not Archbishop Runcie reminded the opening press conference that Archbishop Fisher (a former headmaster of an English public school) closed the 1958 Conference with the words 'class dismissed'? Or were these the married daughters (as Archbishop Runcie had described the United Churches of India on a recent visit) coming home to visit mother to reminisce on their activities since they left home?

Underneath all this, one could not help but be impressed by the sheer energy of the Anglican Church over the last 250 years. Here were men and their wives descended from slaves transported from Western Africa in British ships, from convicts transported from England to Australia, from those who had rebelled against the rule of George III, from those who had called his descendant Empress of India, from those who in the nineteenth century had been colonies of Spain, of France, of Belgium or of Germany. How did they see themselves as they entered this mother church of the city that was within living memory the heart of the Empire that ruled many of them in East and West Africa, East and West Asia, the West Indies and the Pacific?

These were not colonists reporting home to the religious temple in the financial capital of the Empire. The Archbishop of Central Africa, Khotso Makhulu, though himself holder of a British passport and married to an English woman, soon put paid to that idea in his sermon. The service was a celebration of the 200 years of European settlement in Australia. Archbishop Makhulu raised awkward questions about racism against the Aborigines and about racism in Europe. God waits and weeps, he said, over the victims of the world's greed and selfishness. 'What hope is there for the poor nations, when soup kitchens have to be opened in the rich industrialized nations where poverty is growing?' God weeps over the refugees and migrant workers who find it harder and harder to get asylum in European countries; over Aborigines in Australia whose much longer history has been largely ignored in the bicentennial celebrations and whose grievances 'have not been addressed. Perceived injustice, true or not, cannot be wished away'.

At a plenary session called by the African bishops, Bishop Peter Hatendi of Zimbabwe declared to the Church of England, 'We do not want you to be our mother—be our sister.' It became clear that the African bishops owned the Conference as *theirs*. 'This was *my* Lambeth, this was *our* Lambeth' said Archbishop Manasses Kuria of Kenya. It was most important for these bishops to bring their concerns to the attention of Lambeth. At the same time, they raised awkward questions in plenary debates about the sale of English churches to Muslims, and strongly opposed the resolutions of North American bishops on the rights of homosexuals.

The reality was that the procession represented a major success. The world-wide mission effort emerging from the Church of England and its earliest offshoots in North America and the Antipodes, and from chaplaincies and voluntary missionary societies, had produced a world-wide communion of national churches with a strong sense of their own individual identity while thinking of themselves as members of a family.

St Paul's and the Palace—Church and state

Here were bishops with a strong sense of their own identity and the contribution of the Church to the life of their nation. While the Lambeth bishops were attending the opening service of the Conference in Canterbury Cathedral, Bishop Muge of Eldoret in Kenya was being harassed at a church service in his diocese. The Kenyan *Daily Nation* of Friday 15 July had as a banner headline 'House Condemns Muge's Activities'. It then reported: 'Parliament yesterday condemned Right Reverend Alexander Muge, the Anglican Bishop of Eldoret, accusing him of trying to destabilise the country, and called on other church leaders to disown him.' Bishop Muge had warned of tyranny, despotism, violations of human rights, and starvation in East Africa in a diocesan workshop on 27 June.

Bishop Muge identifies his role in Kenyan society, where Anglicans form only 6 per cent of the population, in the following way: 'Most of our countries in Africa have one political party. All opposition has been muzzled. People look at the Church as the only institution which can speak for them, for the oppressed, for the poor. When people come to me and tell me what they are going through, I take it upon myself to take it up. In Kenya, people take very seriously the bishops of the Church of the Province of Kenya.'

Archbishop George Browne of West Africa concurs: 'The Anglican Church has been the only institution that can speak freely, and the people recognize it.' The Anglican Church has produced such figures as Alexander Muge, Khotso Makhulu and Archbishop Desmond Tutu. Bishop Philip Le Feuvre of St Mark's Diocese, South Africa feels the episcopal structure produces personalities who can stand on a platform and give a lead; a lead that people in Africa are prepared for and look to. In many cases, these bishops are the only group who speak for the masses of the people in calling their governments to account. Those who continue the heritage of William Temple in issues of Church and state in 1988 are African.

This prophetic role in the state is not confined to Africa nor to the making of public statements. Archbishop David Leake strongly affirmed the perception of the Latin American indigenous Indian population in Northern Argentina that, had it not been for the 'Misiona Anglicana', they would have been wiped out as a separate people. Bishop Pat Harris identified the Anglican Church's work of providing radio programmes in their own language as a vital factor in giving them a sense of pride in their own culture, their own identity and significance in the national scene, at a time when the military junta were doing everything to absorb them into the mainstream culture.

Here then in St Paul's, leaders of the Anglican Communion demonstrated that within the historical context of imperialism, the gospel of Jesus Christ had brought a strong sense of identity and loyalty—not to the perpetuation of the Empire, nor to the leadership of any mother church, but to living out the gospel of Jesus Christ as national churches in their own right. Indeed the gospel has triumphed, whatever history might conclude about the collusion between colonial, commercial and mission interests. Here we saw evidence for ourselves that the gospel is powerful enough to transcend all such interests. The motives and activities of mission work are not thereby justified or whitewashed. But the gospel transcended all this in British colonialism and broke through all those human structures of global expansion, not just in one culture but in all cultures represented at Lambeth. The power of the gospel can transform. The gospel was taken to the marginalized people. And though it was in many ways an unworthy vessel, the Anglican Church was still a vessel and a channel for the inbreaking of the gospel into many cultures.

These leaders came with the concerns not just of their Christian flock but with the aspirations of the masses in their nations for justice, which they regularly voiced in dialogue with the state. Their witness demonstrates that the heritage of Anglicanism is not to be an acquiescing lackey of imperialism as some histories make it out to be. While Anglicanism did not overthrow imperialism, it made much of it bearable for those who had no prospects of removing it.

The Anglican Church in the non-white colonies provided the context in which bishops who were both leaders in the Church and the nation emerged. An important and symbolic figure of this process was Bishop Samuel Crowther of Nigeria who, in 1864, was made the first black bishop of modern times. He was a freed slave. His potential was seen and encouraged and he was given leadership of a church. He constantly talked about being a national church. He sought to develop the local people and took his role as one of representing the whole of the nation. He saw his role not just as a bishop of his flock but also sought to develop his nation. He promoted policies of the Bible and the plough. He encouraged the growth of plantations. He especially sought to enable the poorer people to break the bond of oppression and slavery through agricultural development. He took important initiatives in contextual theology and liturgy. It was Anglicanism that developed such a leader. All this happened not in the twilight of the colonial era but at its very height. The model he set was not widespread in the colonial era. His own work made such an impact that the next generation of missionaries from Cambridge to Nigeria undertook to take back the control of the Nigerian church into Western hands. It has taken almost a century for the Nigerian church to recover the heritage of Crowther that was removed from it in this way. In this century Bishop Azariah of Dornakal in India was another such figure.

The emergence of the national church

The Anglican Communion became a reality with the emergence of an autonomous episcopal church in the United States. Other national churches followed, beginning with New Zealand in 1857. The emergence of the national church in the Two Thirds World in white colonies is a twentieth-century phenomenon. Independent Anglican provinces were formed in China in 1928, India in 1930, West Africa in 1956, East Africa in 1958 and Uganda in 1960.

These national churches defined their identity as the Church of the nation. They were the Church of India or of Burma, *not* the Church of England in those countries. Their self-designation showed that they saw themselves as national churches. They exercised autonomy as national churches, restricted not by ecclesiastical constraints but by political ones. Even in colonial times here was a Church that had a strong sense of national identity; and significant power was held in these national churches. Instead of mimicking the colonial pattern, the Anglican Church set a model of largely independent churches in a mainly colonial context. It was a commonwealth prior to the British Commonwealth. Unlike the original British Commonwealth, it was not restricted to the white colonies but to the communion wherever it was found.

Did you impress the Queen?

A garden party at Buckingham Palace took place the same afternoon as the service at St Paul's. Shortly after the formalities had begun and while the 'first division' royal team of the Queen, the Duke of Edinburgh, the Prince and Princess of Wales and Princess Margaret were engaged on a walkabout among the guests, a downpour more like an Indian monsoon began, and many scurried for the Palace. Bishops and their wives spent the next hour greeting one another, walking up and down the long red corridor and trying out the sumptuous settees.

Sitting on the Queen's sofas made a great impression on Janet Wesonga from Uganda: 'When you go to other countries and are invited to the house of the head of state, you feel that you have a say in the thought of the country.' She had been introduced to the Queen by the Archbishop of Canterbury as the lady who had preached at the Conference family Eucharist the previous Sunday. 'The Queen asked me "What was your text?" I told her briefly that it was to encourage people to return to the Lord, to join together to share their problems and to join hands with other churches because we all belong to the one Lord. I also thanked the Queen for allowing Princess Anne to come to Uganda because it is not an easy thing to allow your daughter to go where you know there are troubles.'

An interesting royal remark was recorded when one unidentified member of the royal party met a bishop from Latin America and enquired whether he was a Roman Catholic. Was this a gaffe or did it deserve ten out of ten for trying?

What were we to make of this garden party at Buckingham Palace? Was this homage to the ruler? While the Queen is supreme governor of the Church of England and the Archbishop its prime bishop, neither are heads of the Anglican Communion. The Church of England did not make its bishops rulers of the worldwide Church. But it did pass on the close relation between the Church and the state. The Lambeth Conference was not just a gathering of religious leaders. Anglican bishops are also community leaders who have a role in the community. They have this role because the establishmentarianism of the Church of England meant that despite the separation between Church and state in many parts of the world, Anglican Christians had a strong commitment to dialogue with, and relate to, the state. Therefore the visit to Buckingham Palace was not seen as colonial obeisance to the Queen, but as a means of acknowledging the intimate relationship between Church and state which is part of the Anglican ideology and ethos.

One South African bishop pointed out that it was very important for the Queen to receive those who are community leaders. 'I think it was very right and proper that Desmond and Leah Tutu should be received at Buckingham Palace, simply because the Queen as a chieftain should receive another chieftain.'

Leah Tutu had just come from 10 Downing Street, where she with other bishops' wives had expressed a truly Anglican ethos of the relation of Church and state when they presented a petition at 10 Downing Street to ask the British government to meet with those who represented the majority in South Africa. Philip Le Feuvre stated: 'It's important that the blacks in South Africa know that the wife of a white bishop [Mrs Barrington-Ward] was there to present the letter. It will make life pretty difficult for some white rectors in South Africa but they are used to that.'

Philip Le Feuvre also noted that, 'Somebody in our small group was saying that some people in his diocese might be upset to see the Church hobnob with the powerful. But it would have been a breach of hospitality if the Queen as head of the Church of England had not invited the heads of the other Churches to her home.'

The difference in the Anglican ethos can be demonstrated from the situation in Kenya. When the President attends the Pentecostal Church, the leaders offer thanks to God that he is such a holy man. In contrast, while the Lambeth bishops were attending the opening service of the Conference in Canterbury Cathedral, Bishop Muge of Eldoret in Kenya was being harassed at a church service in his diocese because of his criticisms of the government.

There is a track record among some Christian groups to legitimize dictatorships. The Anglican Church in its best expressions has a track record of unwillingness to legitimize political power because, from the very beginning, the state was not a pattern for the structure of the Church. That structure emerged instead out of the inner genius of Anglicanism that each church is nationally autonomous and the bishop and his people have a responsibility to be independent and speak that way. That independence has produced these Anglican churches. That is the Anglican genius. So to misunderstand this as an Empire is a complete distortion of the reality. The role of the African bishops at Lambeth is a model of the way that Anglicanism is critical of the establishment. For they turned on the international gathering of their own fellow bishops precisely the critical intimacy that the Anglican ethos had given them and in which they had been created and nurtured.

This legacy of Anglicanism was dramatically highlighted when the bishops crammed into the crypt of the ancient cathedral at Canterbury for a special performance of T.S. Eliot's *Murder in the Cathedral*. As Bishop David Gitari of Mount Kenya East stood at the back and watched the performance, he could not help but reflect that he himself stood in that line of leadership, having once more hit the headlines in Kenya as the object of fierce criticism by the political rulers of his own nation.

This critical attitude came out of a national identity, the fact that the Church is autonomous, orders its own life, is independent, and must take responsibility for its own situation. If the Church ever thought of itself as that which gets its orders from a mother church outside its national boundaries, this kind of leadership would hardly have emerged. The bishops therefore came to Lambeth as leaders of national churches. The Africans cut confident figures, coming from churches that are growing and have a strong voice in the councils of the nation. Yet they themselves represented a variety of traditions. There were religious traditions of High and Low Church. There were different traditions of relations with the state. The Ugandans came divided among themselves on their stance with relation to their government. They differed substantially from the Kenyans on the issues of the pastoral care of polygamists. Communications in Africa are so difficult, and visa restrictions so complex, that one of the most important aspects of Lambeth for the African bishops was that it gave them a chance to meet one another.

Guests to the end

In contrast to the confident Africans, the Asians were more reticent and seemed to remain on the sidelines of the Conference.

The Asian voice was largely silent at Lambeth 1988. This was a great disappointment to those who had worked hard for the inclusion of bishops from the United Churches of India, Bangladesh and Pakistan to be present for the first time ever since Church union in South Asia as full members. Even in the plenary debate on inter-faith issues, no Indian bishop made a contribution. Such silence was puzzling until one of them gave us a clue: 'We are guests here, that has been made very plain.'

Here was some clear cultural miscommunication. At the beginning of the Conference it had been stressed that the bishops were the personal guests of Robert Runcie (one bishop noted that the bank account for the Conference was entitled 'The Archbishop of Canterbury's Lambeth Conference'); that Lambeth had no legislative role (no doubt to soothe concerns for provincial autonomy); and that the atmosphere was one of personal relationships not legislative formalities. All well and good. In Eastern culture, the guest takes a passive role. He or she participates and comments only when invited to. Therefore the obligation is on the host to invite participation. The needs of the guest are anticipated; the host drops everything to fulfil these needs and to enable the guest to participate fully. In that sense, the presence of the guest, his concerns and needs become the agenda for the host. The guest will continue to remain passive until he is invited to participate, or until his status is redefined.

When it was announced that the bishops were guests, Asians inferred that their expectations would be anticipated and catered for. Yet, during the Conference, as great energy was spent on issues relevant to the Western Church, very little effort was made to identify and highlight the Asian agenda. The Asians suffered this frustration in silence. Africans, with the strength of numbers, forced their agenda to be made public. Further, guests do not take initiatives, nor do they criticize the host—at least, not publicly. So the Asians watched from the sidelines.

Most Asian Christians are in small minorities and this reinforces their identity. Their identity is worked out not only culturally but also in the context of other religions. Indian Christians, for example, are in a situation where if you are a Christian, your loyalty as an Indian is in question. A Hindu's loyalty as an Indian is not questioned, but a Christian's is. Again, you can be Islamic and Chinese, but the saying goes, 'One more Christian, one less Chinese'. The moment a Chinese became a Christian he became a foreign devil.

It is against that ethos that the question is being asked: 'What does Anglicanism mean for us?' Asian Anglicans accept they have an Anglican identity. But they do not want Anglicanism to define them in such a way that they are just an Asian version of Church of England Christians. They want to be *Asian* Christians who have grown up in the Anglican tradition, have shaped it and have become part of it. But it has not given them their primary identity. They are not absolutely sure how to work this out. On the one hand, in Singapore the Anglican Church destroyed a holy table with a figure of a dragon on it. On the other hand, some Indian Christians experiment with styles of worship that some consider as Hindu. It appeared that at the top of the Asian agenda was the question of the meaning of Anglicanism for Christians of the Two Thirds World.

The South Asians who had returned after many years wanted to make sure that this was not the Empire in another form. They were also conscious that their identity was more episcopal than Anglican. This appeared to have reduced their participation. But the South Asians from the United Churches in India and Pakistan had come with a lot to give, especially in the area of ecumenical relations. The Church of South India was formed in 1947 as a union of Anglicans, Methodists of British and Australian origin, Presbyterians, Congregationalists and Reformed traditions. The Church of North India was formed in 1970, bringing together Anglicans, British and Australian Methodists, British Baptists, Brethren and the Disciples of Christ. The Church of Pakistan included Anglicans, Presbyterians, Congregationalists, American Methodists and the Lutherans, the latter two having not joined the Church of South India or the Church of North India.

While the Conference discussed the unity we want to achieve, the Indians wanted to share about the unity they already enjoyed. We talked with three North Indian bishops together, of whom one had begun his Christian life as a Baptist. They shared their aspirations with us:

'We came with our gift, the gift of unity that we have. I wish there was a forum so that we could share this experience, a plenary on unity.

'The unity we have achieved is something very dear to us. We have experienced the joy of having it. By becoming a union we have not lost our episcopacy or our catholicity. We have become more Catholic because we have become fuller in our life of the Church. So we have not become any less Anglican.'

Bishop Sundar Clarke of Madras commented, despite being the fifth generation of Anglican priests in his family, 'I have lost my smaller identity for a larger identity. I have lost my denominational identity. I have gone one step ahead in taking in not only the Anglican tradition, but also the richness in other traditions. The gift the Anglican tradition brought to this was episcopacy, the whole idea that the bishop is the spiritual father to his flock, he is the chief shepherd.'

A bishop from North India commented: 'The Church of North India is not only a United Church but a Uniting Church. Wherever a greater fellowship is possible we will never deny it. We will accept it. We are happy that at least six of us were invited from the Church of North India and we have said that if this fellowship has to be strengthened and continued we would like full representation of the Church in India. The moderator of the Church of Pakistan also requested this strongly. But though we are in communion with the Anglican Church, we are not an Anglican Church. That is why we wore our own distinctive episcopal robes of white cassocks in order to keep our identity.'

Why did the Indian bishops not request a plenary to share their lessons on unity? 'We do not want to impose our will on the Church because we are not fully represented here as yet. This is the first time that we are attending the Lambeth Conference. We do not know how they make up the agenda or who decides who is going to speak.' The loss was not only in the area of unity, but also in liturgy, because the mother of all new liturgies in the Anglican Communion is the Book of Common Worship of the Church of South India.

The Latin Americans were also quiescent in comparison with the Africans. Like the Asian churches, they come from minority situations. Bishop Onell Soto, from Venezuela, commented on the contrast with the World Council of Churches where Two Thirds World leaders have a more visible role: 'In the World Council, all the Churches are members. Here you are guests in a way.' Even some African bishops were also aware of being guests. Peter

Hatendi of Zimbabwe told us: 'We are guests in a very real sense. We have been invited to the Conference and that is wonderful, as guests, and in our culture you have to be polite.'

The pitfalls and perils of partnership

Many of the bishops come from contexts where their countries are economically struggling. Some of their countries are very dependent on the current economic order. And yet, in their persons and stance they demonstrated a firm independence. But the issue of financial dependency could not be overlooked for too long. It forced itself on to the plenary floor.

The bishops of Francophone Africa brought a resolution which called for the Anglican Communion to assist them in their need. The Ugandan bishops convened a special meeting to confer with their financial partners in mission and development agencies about how to make their church financially secure.

Bishop Sydney Ruiz of Brazil told us how since 1973 he had turned his diocese around by asking most of his priests to take other jobs to provide for their support; the diocese only pays the salary of the bishop and two full-time ministers, and pays 50 per cent of the other ten priests' salaries. 'Our church was started in 1890 by two missionaries from the United States,' he said. 'In 1907 we became a missionary district of the Episcopal Church until 1965. But we were financially dependent on the North American church until 1983. But from 1972 we had a ten-year plan to reach financial independence. It was not very successful because we got ourselves into the situation that some priests had to leave the priesthood because the church could no longer pay them. Those who stayed had to take work outside as well to provide for their support. The difference between then and now is that we are aware of our own potential; we decide about our own life; we manage our own financial resources. Previously we had to spend whatever was in the budget for a particular item, say travel, within the fiscal year, otherwise the budget would be cut the following year.'

He also transformed his partner relationship with a North American diocese whereby the North American diocese had been a bank and a tourist agency: 'We are now starting a diocesan companionship committee with a diocese in the United States. Previously our partner diocese was a bank, providing us with money, and a tourist agency sending us visitors. I have now insisted that if people come to visit us, we will have our hearts and arms wide open to receive them, but what we want is the exchange of experiences at different levels. So our diocesan treasurer will contact their diocesan treasurer, our president of the diocesan council will contact their's. They are sending a group at the end of August to get to know us, and to meet our diocesan committee. Then in 1989 we are going to visit them. So we are not just looking to them as a source of money.'

We are aware that Lambeth is a theological Conference with its focus on the faith of the Church. But matters of partnership were also on the agenda as integral to the faith of the Church. Struggles and stories like those above did not catch the imagination of Lambeth—though these were some of the most important contributions that bishops from the Two Thirds World could bring to the Conference. It seemed that the culture of the Conference was dominated by the culture of the code of the English gentleman, who does not talk about money.

For us, it was clear that a number of bishops from the poorer world were keen to address the issue of the Churches' economic dependency on the West. For example, the Ugandan church felt aware that, while its courageous witness was appreciated, it was still an embarrassing experience to be so economically dependent on the West. The economic dependence of the Two Thirds World bishops influences their sharing in several ways. While the growth and excitement of what God is doing in the Two Thirds World can be shared with a tremendous degree of confidence, as that encourages the Church in the West, a critique of partnership cannot be shared because of this kind of economic dependence. They are aware that that is their Achilles' heel. As part of a poor nation, it is here they are vulnerable to criticism.

Christians in the West are also hindered in experiencing the fullness of partnership due to this economic dependence. While they appreciate the spiritual success of the Two Thirds World Church, because of its economic dependence they question the validity of its experience and its relevance to the life of the Church in the West.

Dependency also hinders creativity. Creativity requires the confidence that you can take a line even if it looks totally unworkable. Creativity depends on risk. If your context is one of insecurity, you can hardly afford to add extra risks on top of the already risky situation. For example, as we shall discuss later, many Two Thirds World Churches have not been creative in the area of liturgy. This is understandable. For being in a situation of risk, they do not want to add the further risk of alienating their own people. One reason why Bishop David Gitari could take a strong line on polygamy is that in his situation he is reasonably secure. His diocese is comparatively well funded in Kenya, a country which, in the African context, is fairly stable.

Similarly because of the security of his situation, a bishop in the United Kingdom can make very innovative, creative, and important comments. Even though some would regard them as outrageous, he will not be misunderstood.

Authentic partnership must replace the context of dependency with the context of creativity. Creativity, even spiritual creativity, is hampered by economic dependence. Spiritual creativity sounds inadequate and impractical when it is not matched by an economic viability. It is no wonder that Uganda still has the 1662 liturgy.

Models of partnership

David Gitari models the effectiveness of providing a creative context. He can dream dreams, set his agenda, make plans, and begin to implement them. The Western Church comes alongside as a partner. His own Church is renewed and his ministry in the partner Churches of the West has credibility.

Bishop John Walker, the first black bishop of Washington D.C., spoke of the journey in partnership that he had travelled with churches in Latin America: 'Twelve years ago, I would see the Latin American bishops and they used to argue that the Latin American Churches ought to be set free. But they couldn't be set free because they did not have the economic growth to be set free. Now, once we accept their budget we give it to them and walk away. We trust God and them to do the best that can be done with that budget, and then they have autonomy. They have everything they need to be a province in the Anglican Communion. They are no longer dominated by the United States where we control the purse strings while they have to be good boys to get what they want. The same thing could happen in Africa. African bishops and archbishops should not be forced to go cap in hand to anybody.

Now they come to England or the United States, looking always for the wherewithal to keep their situations free and open, and they cannot be free and open because there are too many strings attached. There are too many people saying "What have you done with the money I gave you?" The Church is growing in lots of ways in Africa, but I think we have got to cut it loose in the sense that it really becomes a free church, a free Anglican Church, a national church free to do what they want to do. In a real sense let the creativity emerge.'

The issue of dependency even has personal implications. Peter Hatendi of Zimbabwe was very aware that 'most of us have not paid for our passage to the Conference and back home. The final issue of the *Lambeth Daily* pointed out how only 9 out of 27 provinces had contributed to the budget of the Conference.'

Bishop Hatendi felt that it would make a very great difference if his diocese could receive a grant five years before the next Lambeth to be invested and used at its discretion for Lambeth concerns. This would contribute also to them feeling more at home.

Seen against such a background, the strong stances taken by the African bishops at Lambeth take on new significance. They emerged out of the Anglican ethos of being their own persons, exercising an independent and critical stance with relation to the state. They emerged out of a context of financial dependency which inhibits a serious examination of one's context, undermines the credibility of the gospel, and hinders creativity. Those bishops who spoke out had begun to develop forms of partnership which did not reflect economic dependency. That is why it was so tragic that Lambeth did not address itself foursquare to this issue to enable others to be released as well.

Notes

1. Since the Conference and at its request the four moderators of the churches where Anglicans have united with Christians of other traditions (in Pakistan, North and South India, and Bangladesh) have joined the Primate's meeting. This brings the proportion to 24 out of 31.

CHAPTER 2

A United Nations
with Evensong

What had they been invited to?

What had the bishops found themselves invited to? In many ways, the Lambeth Conference was the religious counterpart of the United Nations, perceived by bishops in the same way as their national political leaders view that assembly. For the Two Thirds World, the Conference was a vital international global platform. African bishops like Bishop Muge are able to bear a prophetic witness in their countries precisely because their concerns are echoed and affirmed by the Lambeth Conference. The power of the Conference was demonstrated by the reaction in Kenya to an inaccurate report of Bishop Gitari's presentation on polygamy. Reuters put out an incorrect report that the Bishop had allowed polygamy for Christians. Next day, this was front page news in all the Kenyan papers. In his cathedral town of Embu, every conversation in the street was on Bishop Gitari's speech. And President Arap Moi himself issued a strong condemnation of Bishop Gitari's alleged views.

One of the strengths of the Anglican Communion is that it enables the Church in such contexts to undertake its prophetic role. The Anglican Church in the Two Thirds World needs the strength of its global relationships and Western partners to fulfil much of its prophetic ministry. Archbishop George Browne of West Africa notes: 'We are strengthened if we can go back and say that these are the views of the communion. We need that to strengthen us. Whereas those in the West do not need to go back to their countries and say "The Africans agree with us". This is the difference between the individualism of the West and the co-operativeness you find in Africa. The Anglican Church in Africa, for some strange reason, has been the more vocal of the Churches.

They all look to see where the Anglican bishops move, so that we can go back and say that we take this stand which has the support of the rest of the Anglican world. This is not true of any other denomination in Africa.'

The Anglican Communion gives such leaders massive clout. It is for this reason that the Episcopal Church in the United States and the Church of England must not allow themselves to become marginalized in their societies, and dismissed as 'Christians with weird ideas on sexual relationships'.

For bishops from North America and elsewhere in the Anglo-Saxon world, Lambeth had no such high priority. Bishops from the United States and England arrived hot-foot and exhausted from their own national conventions and synods. Some continually stressed their provincial autonomy and clearly signalled that whatever Lambeth decided on the ordination of women to the episcopate, they were going ahead anyway. Bishop Charles Mwai-goga from Tanzania was one who had received this impression: 'There are some provinces that have come here with their decided agenda; they have already discussed the issues back home. They have come here in a way to seek for world-wide approval. But whether we say Yes or No, won't change their decision. I wonder if we say No to the American Church about their desire to consecrate women, whether it will make a difference. I'm not so sure.'

President Reagan had a similar attitude to the United Nations. People in developed economies have enough strength to do what they want. They do not need the Two Thirds World.

'Something of a miracle'

All the bishops with whom we spoke, without exception, identified the daily Bible Study in groups of twelve as the highlight of the Conference. 'A formative part and an enriching experience,' wrote one respondent. Bishop John V. Taylor's notes, 'Briefing the Apostles' on the Last Supper discourse in John's Gospel formed the basis of their study. This was a departure from the procedure of the 1978 Conference where there had been formal Bible exposition in plenary sessions.

Yong Ping Chung from Malaysia, chairman of the Anglican Consultative Council, noted: 'The small groups and the Bible Studies especially have helped the success of the Conference. The small group immediately gives the group of people contacts and contact and makes people very comfortable.'

Colin Bazley, from Chile, noted: 'Our Bible Study group is a lovely group, and we've had a very rich communion there, and sharing among people of very different views and that has been good.'

Michael Baughen from Chester, England, said: 'The cosmopolitan input comes over most strongly in the smaller groups. In my group we have a priest from Papua New Guinea—he works with the ACC; a bishop from Nigeria and one from South Africa—as well as a bishop from the Old Catholics in the Union of Utrecht. Then there's me, the lone Englishman, together with an Australian, one Canadian and two Americans. We're working on the theme "Christ and Culture" and it is in these discussions that so much emerges of the differences in other parts of the world. The Nigerians, for example, find it difficult to "wash other people's feet"—as it were—because at home they find that their people very much want them to be the "big men". I lead the group with an hour's Bible Study before we get down to work on our main subject.'

Bishops coming from vastly different traditions discovered each other's commitment to and love of the Lord and developed an appreciation of each other's reverence for him. John Reid of Sydney greatly appreciated three bishops in his group from Iran, the Philippines and Mozambique who had suffered in a significant way. Maurice Goodall would take back to Christchurch, New Zealand, as the significant contribution of Lambeth to his diocese 'the strength of our fellowship based on the Bible Study and prayer'. Colin Craston, vice-chairman of the Anglican Consultative Council, felt that the fact 'that the Conference turned out to be a much better event than many expected beforehand was mainly due to the spiritual basis established in worship, study of Scripture and prayer. It was thus a renewing experience.'

Canon Samuel Van Culin pointed out that the Bible Study groups were not only a nesting place, but a place where enrichment can occur out of the word of God and of the experience of that word in the life of the local church. Ruth Etchells, a consultant at the Conference, summed up the results: 'As Lambeth met, behind the total disagreement about what the Conference might achieve, lay a profound anxiety that the Church had travelled so far from its true roots of faith that the bitter divisions which were shaking it could not be contained even by the strong bonding of the living fellowship of the one Lord Jesus Christ. But there was also a profound certainty that God was at work among us and sufficient faithfulness remained for that work to be received. The certainty prevailed. For as the days went by at Lambeth, all of us experienced something of a miracle; a slow coming together and bonding in the love of Jesus Christ as we sat together, literally day by day in groups of a dozen or so people under Scripture. Each day began with prayer; and then for an hour after breakfast the whole Conference met in groups to read the same passage from St John's Gospel. People openheartedly shared how that reading addressed their different situations and then prayed. Only then, after coffee, did that same Bible Study group go on to address the issues, including the divisive ones.'

The absence from these Bible Study Grops of some bishops and archbishops who were caught up in other processes of the Conference or in external media concerns was noted with deep regret. They had clearly missed something.

Worship

Many bishops thought something was missing from the worship at the Conference. The setpiece formal opening and closing services were held in Canterbury Cathedral and the Australian bicentennial was celebrated in a Eucharist at St Paul's. In the plenary hall, Eucharist was held every morning before breakfast and was increasingly well attended as the Conference proceeded. There was also daily evening prayer and a family Sunday morning service on the middle Sunday. The African bishops asked for and got a twelve-hour vigil of worship and prayer throughout one night-led by Desmond Tutu, and accompanied by a 24-hour fast for solidarity with suffering people.

Some plenary sessions began with a hymn from *Ancient and Modern* (revised yet again) presented by the publishers. But not all brought their books with them, and from the press gallery the singing sounded tired. At noon each day there was a minute's pause for reflection and prayer. Occasional fringe worship was also arranged before morning Eucharist in the style of the charismatic renewal and of the East African revival.

But the official worship programme was 'far too Anglo-Saxon', according to one respondent. 'A greatly controlled Western liturgy was in use. The Holy Spirit was not given much room for free expression except in the sermon', was how Roger Herfft—originally from Sri Lanka and now a bishop in New Zealand—saw it. For another New Zealand bishop, the worship in general was 'dull', with the closing service 'where we wanted to celebrate, appalling, with mostly choir music and disappointing hymns'. Colin Bazley 'found the worship most unsatisfactory, totally passionless. I would have thought that with all the bishops of the Anglican Communion together that the worship would have been of the highest quality, beauty and relevance.' Archbishop David Penman from Melbourne agreed. David Evans from Peru wrote: 'We got a sort of lowest common denominator in form and in song. The wives had a livelier time, I gather. Things were too "decent and in order" for some Third World tastes.'

The formal occasions in Canterbury Cathedral were beyond the hands of the Conference organizers, and kept firmly under the direction of the dean and chapter of Canterbury. For some, the services were masterful expressions of controlled passion, expressed in the beautiful choir renderings. It was passion restrained, channelized, ordered and under check. Passion was visible in the joy on people's faces, uplifted in absorption in something other than themselves, in appreciation of the neat surroundings and impeccable arrangements, with not one footstep or beat out of place, and deeply moved by the historic nature of the place and the occasion. Particularly striking symbolism was achieved at the closing service at the dedication of the 'Compass rose'—the badge of the Anglican Communion let into the floor in front of the nave altar. Primates stood at five points of the compass to pray in their own language for the needs of the world. The best view was from the camera sited overhead and projected on to the television screens, which had been thoughtfully placed high up on the nave walls.

But people were also disappointed that the kind of passion and freedom that they enjoyed in worship in their own contexts was absent. Onell Soto felt that 'the whole affair is very English. From the worship service to the food, to the schedule, everything.' John Walker of Washington noted, 'Music has already made its impact in our worship. The great singers of the United States, these great women who come and perform in my cathedral in Washington are just incredible. Jessye Norman is one of the few human beings I know who can stand at a crossing in a cathedral without a microphone in sight and fill the entire building with her voice.'

For the bishops from the Two Thirds World, passion is seen more as unrestrained worship. Roger Herfft told us: 'One of the things I missed at Lambeth was that in my rural diocese in an isolated part of New Zealand where the renewal movement has had an impact on Anglican worship, we are freer, we are not bound to the text or to history in such a way that it oppresses. A major shift needs to happen in the Church towards worship in the context of mission. As a Church we do not believe we are in a mission field. Worship must enhance the spirit of mission. For us in the Anglican Communion in New Zealand that has happened. We are far more free. It does not mean we are anti-liturgy. Liturgy is itself a work of the people. But I think that there has been a totally different atmosphere here. Many people still believe in the church as a theatre, where we sit almost as in a railway carriage, one behind the other. The Church needs to move from that to worship as a community experience. Unless it happens I do not think we can be authentic enough to witness.'

But right at the end of the closing service in Canterbury Cathedral, after the BBC TV cameras (which had been far more intrusive than their ITV counterparts three weeks earlier) were switched off, the passion finally broke through.

As the Archbishop of Canterbury led the procession of primates down through their brother bishops seated facing inward in the nave of the cathedral, one group of bishops started clapping. The applause was taken up spontaneously. It reverberated around the walls of the mother church of Anglicanism, perhaps pleasantly surprised at such behaviour during worship, as a grandparent is invigorated by the youthful innovations of its children's children. The applause did not stop after the Archbishop had gone. Bishops from Uganda passing through the massed ranks of North American bishops beamed like the African sun in response to the warm applause which greeted them. Then came the bishops from South Africa. Hands reached out from the procession to clasp those of friends new and old. Would the English bench be able to take this warm display of love and affection? They did, even if their pace did quicken towards the west doors. It was the most inspiring part of the whole service. These Christian leaders loved each other in the Lord and wanted to show it as they parted, knowing they might never meet again in this way on earth. What might they have been able to express if they had been given a freer rein in the services themselves?

The issue of worship is important. For the Anglican ethos is bathed in worship. Its tradition is one of *Lex orandi, lex credendi*. Here were the bishops, the guardians and upholders of the Anglican tradition at prayer. In their prayer we discover their theology. It was here that the African contribution to the Conference was not as full as it should have been. For the Africans, by and large, have not produced Anglican liturgies of their own. In 1978, the Nigerian bishops were the only ones to lead the worship using the 1662 prayer book in English. In 1988 they produced a service which was a translation of the Church of England Series III liturgy with minor adaptations. After Lambeth, Vinay Samuel visited the Province of Nigeria. He discovered there that the form of worship is for the priest to lead the prayer book service (1662) for 45 minutes. After that, lay leaders take over for a time of exuberant and lively worship, sometimes lasting over two hours. There seems to be no real link with the preceding 1662 worship or with their own cultural tradition. But what is Anglican or what is African about their worship?

The Africans did introduce one item of worship into the Conference which made a great impact. They asked for an all-night vigil and a 24-hour fast as a mark of solidarity with the suffering people of the world. In many African Churches the vigil is used as part of the mourning and funeral rites. But the vigil is still not seen as Anglican in many areas. The effect of it being held at Lambeth was to give it a seal of approval as Anglican.

The celebration of the 1000th anniversary of the baptism of Prince Vladimir of Kiev (and thus the millennium of the Russian Orthodox Church) in the nave of Canterbury Cathedral also demonstrated another form of worship. Everyone stood for over an hour and burst into spontaneous applause three times.

Even though the daily worship had variety through being led by bishops from different provinces, sometimes in different languages, the greater impact on people's lives was made by the Bible Studies.

The lack of creative liturgies from Asia and Africa was one of the main reasons why the worship did not have a great impact on the Conference.

Worship was also lacking in the plenary presentation of the women's cause at Lambeth. This is all the more surprising since much of the argument about the ordination of women is about their role in leading worship. The women's cause was put forward as a cerebral case, not as a worshipful presentation of the contribution women bring to the worship of the Church. Yet the Anglican way of presenting something is in worship. Why was this not done?

Debates and decisions

Of course, a major part of the Conference programme was debates and decisions. How did the Two Thirds World view this process? Some were very taken aback by the rules of engagement announced at the first session. Apparently they were being asked to make up their minds before they heard the debate. For they were called on to identify which side of the motion they wanted to speak on, by lining up at seats by microphones either on the left or on the right of the hall.

Peter Hatendi of Zimbabwe found that the very presentation of the material in the form of resolutions to be argued about meant: 'You are already fighting. But if you open it up as a conversation, which is the normal way we do it, asking, "What do you think about this?", you are not defining or defending a position. It is not, "Stand on the right", "Stand on the left", where you are fixed to one side of an issue, defend that and tend to underplay the other side. That does not augur well for a very meaningful and good relationship.'

Onell Soto from Venezuela agreed: 'It is difficult for Third World people to get involved in much of the discussion except in small groups. The reason is that you have to be a Parliamentarian to really stand up in front of 700 people and argue and debate one of the resolutions. You may have an opinion but it takes more skills than that to do that. In many of the churches from which we come, these decisions are made in a different way, through consensus. We talk, and talk, and talk. Here the system is that on the very first day of debate, the Archbishop, instead of saying, "We are going to discuss this", says, "Those who wish to speak *for* will be on this side, those who wish to speak *against* will be on the other side."

This is one of the problems that Third World bishops have at this conference. We need more training in the way that business is conducted in the English way, for, if I am to be in this system, I need to know the rules.'

Were the rules explained adequately? In our survey from the press gallery of those who proposed the motions before the Conference, we noted that the resolution on Iran was presented by a North American, on Namibia by an English bishop, on interfaith dialogue by an Englishman, on Roman Catholic relations by an English bishop, and on the issue of international debt by a Canadian. These proposing speeches were the main speeches on the resolutions. Though this expressed an admirable 'bearing of one another's burdens', we asked Bishop Soto whether he would have been able to present a resolution in this system: 'I do not know, nobody asked me. I did not push for it either,' he replied. Emmanuel Gbonigi of Nigeria describes what (by default?) happened: 'Our section discussed that it would not help if we allow people from Britain, America, Canada, Australia and maybe New Zealand to present the resolution. We should allow people from other parts of the world to present the resolutions. It happens that the secretary of the group is from Australia and the leader is from Nigeria. When the secretaries were asked to go and put finishing touches to the resolutions, we found that the names of the secretaries were put down as the names of those who were going to present the resolutions. In our group we decided that we would not ask the secretary to present the resolution.'

A senior bishop from Nigeria was upset at the timing of the Archbishop of Canterbury's intervention in a debate before it was even half over. In his country, the president of an assembly never gives his opinion until the very end of the debate. His task is to try to summarize the view of the whole body and his view will not be opposed. The interventions by Archbishop Runcie made him feel that the whole process was a *fait accompli*. 'If he had done that as president in my country, we would have censured him,' said the Nigerian.

We put this perception to Archbishop Runcie who gave us this reply: 'In planning Lambeth we were at pains to simplify debating procedures as much as possible, and to be free of a complicated burden of standing orders. We were keen that bishops used to non-parliamentary ways of taking decisions should not feel intimidated, but free to speak their minds in their own way. At the same time, we could not manage such a volume of business without some system designed to give everyone a fair chance to speak. And as president, it was my responsibility to be sensitive to this question, to sense the mind of the Conference, but also to give my own view clearly and firmly, and to take a personal lead where necessary.'

People adapted to this regime in their own way. One English bishop openly admitted to his small group that he would manipulate the process to get his wishes. His method of operating was to put forward something outrageous, allow people to modify it, and then in the end to get what he wanted all along. The Bishop of London, in the debate on the ordination of women to the episcopate, tried to line up a whole series of positions together— faithfulness to Scripture, ordination restricted to men, faithfulness in monogamous marriage—contrasted with a package deal of sitting loose to revelation, ordination of women to the priesthood, and laxity over discipline on sexual morality. One bishop from Pakistan felt there was a clear lesson from the process about the timing of public debate on contentious matters: 'Once people are entrenched in their positions, no public debate will actually help solve the problem. The time for public debate is when people are still thinking through their position. Once they are entrenched in their positions, public debate only makes them take that position more strongly. Something that Lambeth taught us quite clearly is that in Christian circles we do not listen to each other.'

The perspective from the Two Thirds World appears to be that people should not entrench their positions until engagement has taken place. While each bishop was urged to 'bring his diocese with him', preparation for such international gatherings has to be carefully nuanced so that while provinces debate the issues beforehand, they regard the debate as unfinished until they have heard the views of those from other parts of the world. They would do better to come with suggestions rather than with conclusions. If communion means anything, on some issues it should mean that people do not come with decisions. They should come with their discussions, think through a lot together and try to share their positions. They should take the stance: 'I do not think we will make up our minds until we have met with the others.'

For Bishop Pat Harris, formerly of Northern Argentina, the issue was different perceptions of time: 'More time needs to be given to allow people to come out with the issues that they really wanted to discuss. The agenda was already written and had to be completed in a set time. Therefore all the processes and resolutions had to be in by a set time. People are pressurized, and therefore all the issues that they have wanted to bring are not dealt with, because there is no time as everyone moves on to the next thing. People from the North are used to this and are geared up to it. People from Latin America do not work that way. The Indian Bishop in my former diocese in Latin America was invited to this Lambeth, but declined because on his first visit to England in 1984 he had found that he was always being pushed on to the next thing. There was never time actually to finish a conversation or some particular ministry. It was always "you have got to get the train now, move somewhere and do this". He said, "You haven't got the time. Therefore if I am talking to somebody and I want to minister to them, everything has to wait. I find it very disturbing. When I am talking to somebody I finish that, and only then, even if it is a day later, I move on." Perhaps we should have three days of regional meetings for people to discuss their agenda and then give their regions a three-hour plenary with discussion, and only then allow the agenda to be set which would be completed very quickly.'

Confirmation of Pat Harris's view comes from the actual way the Africans handled their own agenda at the Conference. They held regional meetings in Africa in Limuru in 1987. They met in Cambridge prior to Lambeth and issued the Cambridge Declaration. They saw that the issues they were concerned with were not going to be dealt with on the Conference agenda, so they made representations to the Archbishop of Canterbury. Archbishop Manasses Kuria reports: 'We said we did not want to be influenced by others or be rubber stamps. "We are not only Anglicans, we are Africans." So we were granted a special session. As a result, other areas asked for a special session and also regional meetings continued throughout the Conference. These had not originally been planned.'

The African bishops held three regional meetings, formed a subcommittee to work on resolutions that dealt mainly with pressing issues in Africa, and submitted a large number of resolutions to the plenary. These were passed quickly—almost too quickly for some observers, who interpreted the lack of debate in plenary as representing a lack of seriousness. But Manasses Kuria was in no doubt in Nairobi a month after Lambeth that those resolutions would be taken most seriously and implemented, 'because they were *our* resolutions', and because of the process by which they had emerged.

Archbishop George Browne gave us insight into some of the discussions within the African region. He had been ready to oppose the motion on polygamy but saw that many of his African colleagues wanted it for pastoral reasons. Bishop Misaeri Kauma of Namirembe, Uganda, strongly opposed the polygamy motion in the plenary session, but his concern for proper discipline was taken into account in an amendment.

In contrast, one face of provincial autonomy worn proudly by some was a form of placarding of positions by interest groups who said, 'We are going to do this anyway, try and stop us.' Such theology by interest groups does not really work. This is an area where the Africans, Asians and Latin Americans have a vast amount to teach the communion about what communion means.

CHAPTER 3

Bring Your Diocese with You

The Archbishop of Canterbury did not invite his guests to bring their experts or their star theologians with them to sort out the problems of the Anglican Communion. Instead, he invited them to bring their dioceses. In our conversations with bishops, they frequently underlined this aspect of the invitation. Bishop Peter Hatendi of Zimbabwe stressed that the reason the African bishops asked for a special session to share their concerns was that 'we should make concrete the request of the Archbishop of Canterbury that each bishop should bring his own diocese. We from Africa brought our dioceses with us, and we thank the Archbishop of Canterbury for giving us the opportunity to share the concerns of our dioceses. It is part of the nature of this Lambeth conference.' A bishop comes as the focus of the unity of his diocese, and in some senses embodies the life of his diocese.

This invitation shaped the way in which the bishops saw the Conference. This was not to be a big theological exercise or a gathering of prickly theological prima donnas, but of people charged with oversight of large groups of Christians who, in their role, had a corporate personality. Bishops tended to bring to the fore the stories and experiences of their dioceses—the problems of violence in Northern Ireland, the combined work of Anglican and Roman Catholic bishops in Liverpool, the suffering of the Church in Iran, the careful diplomacy in the Middle East, and the encounter with fundamentalist Islam in Nigeria, Sudan and Malaysia.

In response to the invitation, David Leake, presiding bishop of the Southern Cone of Latin America, had undertaken a thorough survey of his clergy and laity's encounter with Roman Catholics, and of some Roman Catholics' views of Protestants. Unfortunately he then found himself in a section and group that did not have this as an issue to address.

However, by asking the bishops to bring their dioceses with them, the Archbishop of Canterbury changed the nature of the Conference. The focus was on the dioceses and the relation of the bishops to them, not on personalities. The door was opened to the Africans to bring their dioceses genuinely to people's attention. It opened the door for the Two Thirds World contribution as nothing else had done and provided an opportunity for them to share the life of their dioceses. It opened the Conference members up to a different way of relating to each other. Lambeth 1988 was an encounter of dioceses, not just of bishops.

For in reality, the road to doing authentic theology lies in reflection on the witness of the people of God in real-life situations. We thank God that the Conference was not dominated by theologians, and those who cross every theological *t* and dot every *i*.

In this way, Lambeth '88 set out far more of the reality of the Anglican Communion than had previously been possible. The invitation clearly set the balance in favour of those engaged in practical mission and ministry. For some bishops, it had to be asked whether they would be able to bring a diocese to which any significant number of Christian believers belonged, or whether they would dare to bring a diocese which hardly had any recognizable Christian identity. Or were they bringing their own personal idiosyncrasies? Some bishops were still caught up in trying to take part in a Lambeth Conference that belongs to the history books, hopefully swept away for ever by Robert Runcie's master stroke in inviting them to bring their dioceses.

This exposure to the world-wide Church through its leaders who brought their dioceses made a profound impact on the bishops. Bishop Sundar Clarke of Madras was moved at the Sunday morning family service halfway through the Conference by the sight of all the African bishops on the platform, coming from different countries, with different views, tensions and conditions, but all united in Christ. He was 'overwhelmed with and caught up in the whole Lambeth atmosphere, which is of such a sense of the universality of the people of God as I have never felt anywhere before'. Bishop Clarke was particularly touched by the comment of Bishop Alexander Malik, the moderator of the Church of Pakistan, that 'it is only at a conference like this that I can be surrounded by Indian brothers'.

Bishop Onell Soto thought Lambeth was wonderful because it involved bishops and their wives from all over the world and made them members of one body. 'It strengthens our faith and fellowship and makes us realize in a tangible and practical way what the universal Church is all about.'

What does it mean to be a bishop?

With this request on their invitation, the bishops came asking, 'What does it mean to be a bishop; how can we be bishops better; how do we deal with our struggles as bishops?' They gave many different answers to the question of what it meant to be a bishop. For Bishop Gerard Mpango of Western Tanganyika, being a bishop meant being hospitable. He gave no appointments and undertook no administrative responsibilities. He just made himself available at a moment's notice for anyone who needed help: 'In Africa, we tend to listen and take time for somebody. As a bishop, I have so much to do and a lot of things are expected of me. But I have no schedule and no appointments. If you want to see me, and you have a genuine need and reason to see me, then you see me. You do not have to go through whatever bureaucracy you have to go through to see a bishop. I am just there in my home or my office, and if people have a really genuine need, they can see me up to ten o'clock at night. I sometimes use my car to take people to hospital because in my rural diocese there are not many cars, and if a lady wants to deliver a baby, and our hospital vehicle is away, sometimes they come and say "Bishop, can you help?" I use that very African response to need. I am available as a pastor and servant to the people.' For Khotso Makhulu, being a bishop meant being a servant as an extension of his previous ministry as a priest. This entailed being willing to serve as a supply priest if necessary.

Indian bishops felt they had received episcopacy in a monarchical form, had reformed it and now have episcopacy in a democratic context where bishops can do nothing in a diocese on their own. They have to act in council. In Nigeria, by contrast, Bishop Emmanuel Gbonigi of Akure, Nigeria, sees the bishop as having a very patriarchal role as father of the tribe: 'In Nigeria, we are very patriarchal, with an emphasis on the father of the ethnic group, the father of the tribe. Something of that concept has come into the people's view of the bishop in Nigeria from their respect for leaders in our culture. They see the bishop as father of the whole diocese. We are trying to change that to get them to centre their attention on Jesus Christ as Lord and head of the Church and to see the bishop as one of the servants. This constitutes a challenge for us to have the grace of God to show the humility not to divide the attention from our Lord and master to ourselves.'

Alexander Muge would like people to see their bishop as a shepherd, as a pastor who is close to his people, not aloof from them, but among his flock and creating closeness with them. Bishop Bashir Jeevan from Pakistan saw his role to be pastor of the pastors, to promote evangelism and to keep the Church united. Sundar Clarke from Madras found his role: 'as a man of the people. I am trying to identify myself with people who are struggling and their problems. I am a village boy. I spend ten days a month in the villages. I am a very pastorally oriented person. I have no enmity or bitterness with people. I just have this gift of putting my hand on everybody, even people who are difficult. I do not think it is any special virtue or merit in me. I think it is just my spiritual responsibility to do so.'

Bishop David Gitari of Kenya had found some of the concepts about episcopacy implicit in the Anglican heritage challenged through evangelistic encounters with nomadic people in northern Kenya. In this case the evangelizers were evangelized. He told the Conference in the plenary session on the Gospel and Culture: 'The "dignity, pomp and regal splendour" of a bishop with his convocation robes or cope and mitre made by Wippells looks absurd to these nomadic people in the Sahel-like part of northern Kenya. The concept of a monarchical bishop who has to exert his authority from his distant residence and who might be seen once every two or three years bears no relation to anything in nomadic culture or experience.

'This prompts us to look for another model of episcopacy that could mean something to the converts. Fortunately, an excellent traditional model is close at hand. Nomadic people enjoy the words of Jesus that "I am the Good Shepherd", and would fully agree with him that the good shepherd "calls his own sheep by name and leads them out". Nomad culture cries out for a concept of a bishop as a shepherd who knows his sheep by name and who makes them lie down in green pastures.

'Gabbra society—and many other traditional African cultures —has something to offer to the Church world-wide as we grapple with such issues as collegiality and authority. Their traditional leadership is collegial, not monarchical. When any important spiritual or secular problem arises, it is solved by the council of elders meeting and sharing their accumulated wisdom. No elder, however well-respected and well-qualified, is permitted to determine a legal or religious question on his own authority.

'One of the most important qualifications for a traditional African leader was knowing when to give up his position. In many societies, the elderly did not expect to hold on to power for ever. At the right moment they stepped aside to make way for the next generation of elders. They did not lose as a result; for society accorded them the very highest honour as elder statesmen. They had earned the right to be respected without having the daily burden of duty.

'Unfortunately this African tradition of leadership has been obscured by a foreign monarchical system. It is hard for some leaders in Africa today, whether leaders of a secular or of a religious organization, to give up power voluntarily. The leaders of the Church in Africa should give a lead in this area, using the gift of discernment to determine when to hand over the mantle of power to others.'

In the Middle East, the bridge between Africa and Asia, Bishop Samir Kaffity of Jerusalem saw that in the Anglican world the episcopacy is shaped by Western concepts, whereas episcopacy is an Eastern concept: 'We emphasize that the episcopate is the sign of unity and leadership. It is the image of the Church in the Middle East. We are living with the ancient churches where the figure of the father in God, the patriarch, the bishop is the symbol of unity and oneness. People congregate round such a figure just as they congregated around Christ. It is the same in Islam. People congregate around the imam because he is one part of the community and similarly in Judaism. This is an important and significant role of the episcopate in the Middle East.

'Episcopacy is one of the essential ecclesial characteristics of the Church of God, as found in Antioch, Jerusalem, Alexandria and

Constantinople, the four main sees of Christianity, and much later in Rome. We see episcopacy as an essential form of ministry for the Church which is biblical and connected with the apostolic tradition. That is why we need to consider this matter of women and the episcopate on a world-wide level, and not just as a matter for individual provinces.'

In Latin America, the bishop has been the leader and often the initiator of mission. Bishop Colin Bazley of Chile feels that the bishop has the role as the focus of the Christian community 'since we were there from the start of the Anglican community. So almost every Anglican Christian who has been converted knows us. In a sense, we give the Church a sense of its own history.' In Argentina, Bishop Pat Harris and his successor, Bishop David Leake, travelled around on bicycles. For Pat Harris, a very important part of the contribution of the Latin American Church is its understanding of ministry and episcopacy. He sees that in most parts of the world with a long history of Anglicanism, the form of episcopacy adopted is authoritarian and very hierarchical, because that was true at the turn of this century. The Anglican episcopate was only formed in South America in recent years. The bishop is very much closer to the model of chief pastor. In no way does he see himself as a figure of hierarchy. He has a very simple lifestyle and a very close identification with the community in which he lives. For example, all the bishops are called by their Christian names and would only be called 'bishop' when actually functioning at a particular moment in his work. This shows the recognition that the bishop is the bishop at certain times, but then he merges and becomes one with the rest of the community. This whole area of ministry and episcopacy is not modelled on the hierarchical model of the Roman Catholic Church, which is what is known in the country itself. And for that reason, he thinks there is enormous value in bishops from other parts of the world visiting Latin America and having the opportunity to experience an episcopacy that is of a very different nature.

'I was consecrated as Bishop of Northern Argentina in 1973 in an open-necked shirt and wearing a poncho—not just to be different but because I wanted to establish that it was possible for me as an English person and for the future that you did not have to have all that regalia, and also knowing that the next consecration was going to be of an Indian bishop. Therefore, I wanted him to know he would be in the same line of tradition. It was wonderful that we had the freedom to do this because we were in a context of a colonial past with which we had no connection, and which we could easily distance ourselves from and set ourselves against.'

Bishop Onell Soto saw that 'in Latin America, as in many other places, there is a breakdown in family life. For people to see the clergy and the bishop as a married man who has a family and children, and has all the problems that they have, is an example for the community. People look with admiration and sometimes amazement at him to see a bishop with his wife.

'Since 1971 our bishops have been elected. So I tell my people— I have not been sent from the United States. You people elected me. I believe in really talking and sharing with people. So we make the contribution of a new kind of authority given by service and ministry. This is not authority that comes from the top. Many times the temptation is to apply authority because this is what you see. But I do not sign any cheques. I do not want people to see me as the boss or the employer. People have to know I am a pastor. I have a ministry, but it is not of telling people what to do but of bringing them along. I share with them why I think these are steps we need to take. It takes time, it takes for ever.'

Just as the implanting of the Anglican Church in these different parts of the world had not been on the model of a colony of the mother church but as independent national churches, so the nature of the role of the bishop has taken its own shape in each different context. The Two Thirds World bishops are far from being English- or American-style bishops in a different country. Their role and their relation to their communities vary considerably. There is an increasing pluralism in what it means to exercise episcopal oversight in the Anglican Communion.

The dioceses they brought with them

The context of mission in which each bishop was set came across very strongly, either consciously or unconsciously. It was clear that the context of the bishops from the Two Thirds World was the context of mission, often in situations of enormous pressure.

These contexts were clearly spelt out in the two unplanned plenary sessions on African and Asian issues.

In the Asian evening, a most impressive presentation was made by Bishop Brice of the South Pacific Anglican Council. This includes the Anglican Province of Papua New Guinea, the Anglican Church of Melanesia and the diocese of Polynesia, and covers 200 million square miles. It is made up of small independent sovereign states, all on small islands with the exception of Papua New Guinea. On page 60 of the Anglican cycle of prayer they are shown as small dots above Australia and New Zealand.

Bishop Brice identified three issues and concerns that the South Pacific Anglican Council wished to put before the Lambeth Conference. First, the life and death issues of their region. Second, the needs of their church, and third, their frustrations and joys with the Anglican Communion. Life and death issues were making their people uneasy. The continuing nuclear tests of the French government in French Polynesia threatened their lives and those of their children, and polluted the marine life which was the main source of food for many of the people. They were constantly told that the tests were of no danger to the people of the Pacific islands. If that was true,why were the French not testing these in France itself? Their protests were ignored. The need to improve weapons for the security of France on the other side of the world seemed to be more important than the lives of a few natives in the Pacific.

He continued: 'You may say "How can Lambeth help?" You as Churches have pressurized your governments and multi-national corporations concerning investment in South Africa. Surely the lives of our people are just as important for some reaction from a world conference such as this.

'Secondly, our sea needs protection. We need your people to respect our 200 mile limit. With limited land area which produces limited resources, the sea is an alternative means of supplementing our livelihood. Fishing rights, sea exploration for alternative energy, minerals and other resources need a lot of protection from outside investors who have money and might to do what they want and disregard our needs. For example, a United States fishing vessel was arrested by a Solomon Islands gunboat for poaching in its waters. Uncle Sam used his upper hand and threatened to stop trade and aid with that country. Anglican church leaders from the USA, Korea, Japan and Taiwan need to assist us to watch and respect our 200 mile limit because your countries fish in our waters. Please get people in your churches to influence government policy to stop anything that would spoil our means of livelihood.'

Bishop Brice continued in similar vein and then spoke of his people's frustrations and joys. As a region—not only in the Anglican Communion but contrasted with other world organizations—their smallness in size as countries, as populations and as Anglicans meant that various bodies tended to group them with Asia or Australasia, or as somebody else's appendix. This frustrated the people, and implied that they had nothing significant to offer or share. Their smallness kept them from being heard. It was very frustrating to attend world gatherings in which they were asked to speak and then nothing happened afterwards. Nice things were said about their contributions, but they knew in the end that it was issues that hit the headlines, like the ordination of women and the troubles in South Africa, that would win the day. What many people remembered from the Pacific region was either a man wearing a hat or a woman with flowers in her hair. The life and death issues were nearly always forgotten and many traditional partners tell them to keep away from Russia and Libya. But if their partners do not hear them and they then turn to people who *are* willing to listen to them, they get blamed.

Bishop Brice concluded: 'But we are not in despair. We have our joys. We have the biggest ocean in the world which God has given to make up for our small land. We do not have people dying for lack of food. We have the extended family which makes no one feel left out. We are grateful that we have clean beaches and water that is clean. We are grateful that five to seven minutes of your time in the three weeks in the Lambeth Conference is given to telling you something about ourselves.' Enthusiastic and sustained applause followed.

The story of the Maori Church

The Venerable Yong Ping Chung from Malaysia, the chairman of the Anglican Consultative Council, identified that Asians are very conscious of their roots, of their grandfather, and great-grandfather. 'That is important for us. We may not do exactly the same thing as our grandfather does, but we will remain there.' Bishop Te Whakahuihui Vercoe, the Maori bishop of Aotearoa, New Zealand, brought to the Conference the history of the Church among his Aboriginal people. For the first four decades of the nineteenth century, the Church in New Zealand was totally Maori.

The gospel was brought to their shores by Samuel Marsden from New South Wales. In 1822, the Williams brothers came with the Church Missionary Society and established the Church among the Maori people.

In 1841 the English Church sent George Augustus Selwyn to be its first bishop. New Zealand is the largest Polynesian nation in the South Pacific, but that tends to be forgotten because most New Zealanders are English or of English descent. On his arrival, Bishop Selwyn found the Maori church well established by a number of missionaries, some of whom had by this time secured for themselves the trust and respect of the people among whom they lived and worked. Bishop Selwyn impressed himself on the Maori people by the fact that he was able to preach his first sermon totally in Maori. But he was never able to enjoy the same mutual trust and respect among the Maori as Marsden and the Williams brothers did. After ten years, Selwyn found it was harder than he thought to plant the seed of a new religion in the hearts of the Maori, and harder still to unite the settler church with the Maori church into one single body.

So he turned his attention to such matters as church government, division of his diocese, and writing the constitution of the Province of New Zealand. From this point on, the division between the Maori church and the settler church was to become more evident. The Maori name for the Anglican Church in New Zealand means 'the church of the missionaries', a name taken from their history, and in gratitude for the way the gospel was brought to their shores.

So in their history since 1814, two Anglican churches have grown together, one for the indigenous people, and one for the settlers. That has been maintained right up to the present day, and is why there is a so-called 'ethnic bishop' for the Maori people of New Zealand. The Maori people do not see it that way because their agenda at the moment is to pronounce and proclaim the oneness of the Church within their shores, and so they have undertaken a programme of cultural development and partnership.

'Bi-culturalism', Bishop Vercoe continued, 'is the theory that it is beneficial for two cultures to exist within one nation. This is the opposite of assimilation or integration. We believe we must begin with the development of bi-culturalism within our shores.

'Bi-culturalism can also refer to the ability of a person to embrace two cultures and be at home in both. Until recently, bi-culturalism in this sense has been forced on the Maori people, but not expected of the European. So the Church has undertaken deliberately to marry these two cultures together within the framework of the Church in New Zealand. Bi-cultural development is the process whereby two cultures grow to develop within one nation in the spirit of mutual respect and responsibility. Maori culture and European culture will be encouraged to develop as integral entities but also to overlap. This development recognizes that the majority culture is required to take positive steps to protect and encourage the minority interests and needs. For without such a commitment a minority culture may not be able to survive.'

Bishop Vercoe went on to say that a monument in their largest city, Auckland, was erected at the turn of the century in memorial of the last Maori people. To the amazement of the people who put the memorial up, the Maori population subsequently grew at two or three times the rate of the European population. That memorial stood as a contradiction to what actually happened. Applied to the Church, bi-cultural development meant taking steps to ensure that the gospel of Christ takes root in, and is expressed through, two different cultural forms within the one provincial or national church. It witnessed to the enriching diversity of God's creation, and at the same time recognized the essential unity of all creation in Christ.

'Bi-cultural development', Bishop Vercoe continued, 'is also the process whereby individuals identified with one culture grow in understanding and experience of the other. Such a development for the Christian is an expression of neighbourly love. Partnership requires co-operation and interdependence between distinctive cultural or ethnic groups within one nation. It implies that Maori and European have gifts to give and receive from one another, and nationhood is best established when both partners are valued and respected and share fairly in decision-making and the resources of the nation.

'In the Church, the principle of partnership means that each cultural group or people is accorded the same dignity in Christ, makes their distinctive contribution to the common life of the Church and each supports and encourages the other. There is mutual responsibility and interdependence within the body of

Christ. Both cultural groups are impacted by the influence of each on the other, and a new culture emerges that is neither European or Maori.

· 'New Zealand can be described as one nation with three histories—a Maori history, a European history and the history that we together are now forming and making come into being. The emergence of this New Zealand culture may be the inevitable long-term prospect and we believe this is our goal. We have a Maori proverb which says "With your basket and my basket, together we will feed the multitudes." The Church needs to ensure that its structures encourage respect and justice and that its members put on Christ and show the quality of love with which he loved us, if the principle of partnership is to become truly incarnate in life.'

The story of the Middle East Church

Bishop Samir Kaffity from Jerusalem represented the Anglican Communion in the Middle East. His church has one foot in Africa and one in Asia, and is in a religiously plural context with Islam and the Jewish faith, in a land which has served as the historical platform not only for the foundational events of the Christian faith, but also for working out and expressing the meaning of the faith for generations.

The Anglican Church came in 1841 during the missionary era, when the West felt it had a special mission to the Third World. They carried the Bible concomitantly with the expansion of colonialism like a railway, with two lines going together. Another objective at that time was to convert non-Christians. The third objective was to make a presence and be bridge builders between the Christian churches that had been in existence in the Holy Land since the time of Jesus.

He told us that there was little conversion. An Anglican presence started from the already existing Christians who enjoyed a new form of education produced by the missionary schools and welcomed the Westernization of the area. Thus they joined the Anglican Church. The Anglican Church's immediate roots came chiefly from the missionary societies of the Church of England who were responsible for the Anglican Church in Jerusalem and the Middle East.

Bishop Kaffity continued: 'We are grateful that there is this relationship. Because we were Christians already there. Some of us like myself are third-generation Anglicans. But the previous generations were Orthodox. So we are also conscious of our deeper roots in the area and we are trying to see ourselves as Anglicans in the context of the deeper roots and not just of the immediate.

'Perhaps Anglicans were best in their third objective of building bridges of understanding and reconciliation, bringing together Eastern and Western, old and new Christianity. We feel there is a special role in the motherland of Christianity for Anglicans who have a share in Catholicity and in the Reformation, both theologically, ecclesially and even in their strategy of mission. In that respect, we feel that the Anglican Church in Jerusalem and the Middle East is now providentially placed by God to do this ecumenical bridge-building, understanding, and bringing Christians closer and closer together.

'In the context of two other sister religions, as Anglicans we do not see the Christian faith divorced either from Islam or Judaism. We do not start with the English Reformation or with the secular Renaissance. We start where we are with Muslims and Jews. We have the Hebraic tradition of our faith and the post-Christian tradition of Islam. There is much in common between these three faiths and we like to see them synoptically, together and not comparatively as others like to see them. In this respect we may humbly produce a contribution to the world Anglican Communion in their relations to Islam and Judaism.

'Islam is the fastest growing religion in Europe and the United Kingdom. In some countries it has become the second religion after Christianity. So this experience of the tiny Anglican Church and the Christians in the Middle East of seeing the Muslims as equal brothers, not looking at them paternally, might be a contribution to Christian–Muslim relationships in Europe in the present and the future. We think this is an important task of the Anglican Church in Jerusalem and of the communion. We hope to contribute to this policy of understanding, exchange, dialogue, or rather trialogue, with Judaism and Islam, during this Conference.

'We also may be able to contribute to the thinking of the Anglicans from the rest of the provinces of the world on the burning issues for the life and death of humanity. In Europe and America they speak a lot of the Christian position on the arms race, on cold and hot wars, on all sorts of international conflicts. We in the Middle East have been living for the last 40 or more years in the middle of a very serious international crisis which will have its implications elsewhere in the world. So we cry and plea for justice, peace and equality and for the ending of the arms race and for not using the Third World, and particularly the Middle East, as a laboratory for the experimentation of sophisticated arms produced by the giants who are able to produce arms. We are able to produce a new dimension in the discussions of the Lambeth Conference to give attention and concern in exerting not just pressure but being prophetic to the respective governments in dealing with these issues.'

For Bishop Kaffity it was an embarrassment that his church was seen not only as part of the Anglican Communion, but as part of the Western tradition of Christianity which has left so many sad landmarks in the history of the region. The Crusaders used force and terrorism in their campaign to regain the holy places. The existing indigenous Christians of the Holy Land were embarrassed and appalled. Conversion of Christians in great numbers to Islam took place. But there is enough awareness among the Arabs today that the Christians of the Middle East are theologically, sociologically, and politically seen as an integral part of the Arab world rather than the Western world. Bishop Kaffity feels that that 'part of our contribution to the Anglican Communion is to remind the communion that it is not an English or Western communion. We are not a decoration in the communion, we are as we are part of this communion. We have our kinship and attachment to our own people, especially struggling for justice and peace. In the communities that I serve in the diocese of Jerusalem, the bulk of the Anglicans are Palestinians who are struggling for justice, peace and reconciliation in a way that will give back the Palestinian his dignity as a human being just like his cousin and brother the Israeli. 'The Church in the Middle East is very ecumenically minded. It is in the leadership of the regional ecumenical movement and the Middle East Council of Churches and other structures there. We have been in very serious discussions with the Presbyterians and the Lutherans about going into United Churches and have been interrupted by the wars that took place in Palestine and Israel since 1967 when other agendas took priority. But this is still on. At one time the scheme in Ceylon was thought as one of the most relevant for the Middle East. Now this scheme is being revived slowly. But also there are ecumenical encounters and joint ecumenical sharing in particular with the ancient Churches. The Middle East Council of Churches covers twenty-four countries and all three main families of Churches in the area, the Orthodox family, the Oriental Orthodox family and the Anglican Protestant—with close observation from the Roman Catholics. The question of their coming in is being seriously discussed. They are part of some of our joint projects. Ecumenism is not an academic exercise. We do not write books about ecumenism in the Middle East: we live it.

'Anglicanism is very precious and is seen as the *via media* and the dynamic movement between the Churches to bring them closer and closer together.

'The Orthodox see in us quite a common heritage, especially that we keep the threefold order of ministry and stress the episcopate as a sign of unity. They are worried that if we lose that with the new interpretation of the episcopate by other Anglican Churches, it will present the situation in the Middle East with a serious problem of how to relate.

'The Protestant Churches feel that they can speak and relate to the Orthodox and Roman Catholic through the Anglicans. In the discussions of unity they have given prominence to the concept of the episcopate and episcopacy. It has not been as serious a problem to them as it was for the uniting Churches in the 1940s in the subcontinent of India.'

The context of struggles

We asked Bishop Kaffity what particular Anglican stance and perspectives his Church was bringing to the life and death issues of social witness in the area: the state of Israel, relations with surrounding Arab nations, and the Palestinians.

His first point was that since the Anglican Church is a communion, not a 'super church', there was no Anglican *ex cathedra* statement on these issues. In his province, Anglicans tried to emphasize the dignity and freedom of all people on an equal footing. They would not like to see one people usurp the rights, life and the personality of another. That is why they see themselves engaged in the non-violent struggle for peace and justice between the Palestinians and Israelis.

'The Palestinians', he said, 'have the evident right to determine their own present and future on what remains of their land. That is elementary for peace and reconciliation in the Middle East. They should be treated as such and granted this right which was granted to all other peoples. We are proponents of that kind of a process of peace and justice, not a biased one. We know that the question is complex, that there is a lot of entanglement, even of the use of the Bible in trying to justify this position over against that position; we try to divorce any political use of the Bible, because the Bible remains a Bible, not a political manifesto. It is very dangerous to use the Bible politically; the devil himself will use the Bible. Perhaps he is using it more than the devout and trying to justify corrupt structures in the world.'

Europe and North America

The contexts other bishops came from also became clear during the Conference. For some bishops from North America and Europe the context was the scientific and technological culture. David Jenkins spoke of the difficulties in sharing the gospel that had been shared by Peter and John in Acts in a society where people no longer needed God, to whom God was irrelevant, where everything was questioned, where people had no interest in religion, and where God could not answer any of the questions because all their questions were answered by science.

In the debate on homosexual rights, it was argued by Bishop Spong of New Jersey on television, and by Bishop Moore of New York in a press conference, that the homosexual orientation of people was the result of a chemical imbalance in their bodies for which they were not responsible. This meant for them, a revision of the traditional biblical teaching on homosexuality. It appeared that a judgement of science was being used to redefine scriptural teaching.

But there are other dioceses and other perspectives in the United States. John Walker of Washington spoke of the refugees flowing out of Central America and Mexico: 'Does the Church say, as some Churches in the United States are wont to say, "Let's keep those people out"? One of the proudest moments of my life was to hear the Episcopal Church and the Methodist Church, and almost every church, say, "These people have a right to be here. We will not let them go back to Latin America and be killed. We will give them sanctuary.'' That makes you proud to be a Christian when that happens. These are the kind of issues we feel ought to be addressed at this Conference in the public plenaries, not hidden away in the section meetings.'

These were the dioceses they brought with them: dioceses in Nigeria, under the heel of an international debt of 210 billion pounds to the International Monetary Fund; dioceses in the Sudan, where there was enormous pressure on Christians from the government's intention to enforce the Shariah law; dioceses in Tanzania, where, Bishop Mpango told us, 'We are taking our gospel to be more holistic—to deal with both the spiritual as well as the physical aspects of man. Tanzania is one of the poorest nations in the world, and so if you are a bishop in Tanzania you have to be honest to your calling as a bishop and cannot avoid involving yourself with the issues of poverty'; dioceses in Francophone Africa, in situations of poverty where it is a struggle to pay the salaries of the clergy; dioceses in South Africa, under the heel of apartheid; dioceses in Kenya, where Church leaders are under the watchful and suspicious eyes of the government; and dioceses in Burma, South Korea and Chile, where political upheaval was just below the surface and burst out in the weeks following Lambeth.

These situations impacted the Conference at the plenary sessions, as through presentations and resolutions bishops brought the concerns of their dioceses to the whole gathering. But the concerns surfaced more in the personal sharing between the bishops, especially in the group Bible Studies. Bishop Richard Harries of Oxford, England, wrote in his diocesan magazine after Lambeth: 'Just before we started the Bible Study in my small group at Lambeth, one of the bishops glanced at a newspaper and saw that eight hundred people had been killed in his district in the last month alone. In fact, so fierce is the fighting in his part of the country that he is in exile. Furthermore, when he put forward a resolution urging the need for human rights to be observed (with a reference to his own situation in the explanatory notes but not in the resolution itself), the other bishops from that country prevailed on him to withdraw it, on the grounds that they would be in serious trouble with their government as a result.'

But the media missed all this. These photo albums of their dioceses that the bishops brought with them were not on display for the Church in England. So the bishops had to pack them back in their suitcases, along with their other Lambeth baggage. Had all the stories from these bishops been shared and collected, it would have been enough to fill ten books and to provide, in many ways, a modern-day Acts of the Apostles. A better job seems to have been done at the Wives' Conference, where every province and diocese had a pictorial display set up on the walls of their tent in the grounds of nearby St Edward's School. The plenary hall of the main conference had acres of unfilled space that could have been graced with similar displays.

This situation leads us to reflect that if Lambeth is to continue to be held in the United Kingdom, it must have a greater impact on the Church of England. Some Two Thirds World bishops did of course visit partner dioceses before Lambeth. But the Church of England itself had its own summer synod just before Lambeth began, so the attention of many of the leaders of the host Church was elsewhere and not on the Lambeth bishops. Further, many of the bishops whose dioceses are making the greatest impact and had a lot to share, only had time to fly in for the opening service and fly out immediately after the close. There need to be channels through the Lambeth Conference process whereby the contributions of such people, whose enormous responsibilities in their own dioceses prevented a longer stay, can be communicated to the Church of England. Some also expressed dismay that the timing of Lambeth in the British summer holidays meant that there was little opportunity for visiting bishops to relate to the Church of England after Lambeth, since most of its members were on the beaches of Brighton, Benidorm or the Bahamas, and its own bishops were taking their annual leave.

It would of course have been very difficult for all 500 + bishops to share the stories of their dioceses. It would have been marvellous if each bishop had been asked to share in smaller gatherings the one thing he felt he had to bring from his diocese to share with everybody. The *Lambeth Daily* made a valiant effort by asking a number of bishops to say in one sentence, 'What is the most encouraging thing happening in your diocese or province?' Such a request reflects a culture of 'byte-sized comments' that many thought disfigured the United States presidential election. For what can be adequately communicated in one sentence in answer to such a question?

CHAPTER 4
Evangelism and Mission

Decade of Evangelism

'This Conference, recognizing that evangelism is the primary task given to the Church, asks each Province and diocese of the Anglican Communion, in co-operation with other Christians, to make the closing years of this millennium a "Decade of Evangelism" with a renewed and united emphasis on making Christ known to the people of his world.'[1]

For many bishops, this resolution was the highlight of the Conference. Some felt that it represented a major success for the bishops from the Two Thirds World who pushed for it. One English bishop wrote to us, 'Marvellous about the decade of evangelism; this can be taken back to the diocese as the Lambeth resolve, not as the bishop's private fad.'

The bishops were happy with this resolution, not because they had decided to do evangelism in any new way but because the resolution affirmed what they were doing already. There was no sustained discussion of the issues raised in evangelism in the various contexts from which they came.

In what kind of contexts is evangelism being done?

There were many understandings of evangelism at the conference and some hard questions were raised. For bishops came to the Conference from very diverse contexts, and from very different experiences of evangelism.

Bishops from Asia came from a setting where religion is a dominant force, and where other living faiths are resurgent. Christianity has coexisted for centuries with militant Islam and Hinduism, which is tolerant of everything but intolerance. Professor Stanley Samartha from India pointed out in his plenary address that in Asia, Christians make claims for Jesus in a setting where other religious scriptures also speak with authority. Hindu and Buddhist writings parallel everything that Christians claim with the same degree of theological and philosophical depth, finesse and logic. Apart from Islam, Asian religions tend to be non-aggressive and accommodating. They absorb or confine Christian activities. There is no overt confrontation.

In Malaysia, the Church is growing among tribal peoples in East Malaysia. But in West Malaysia, the Church struggles with the new laws forbidding the use of certain words by Christians, for example, the traditional word used for God, 'Allah'. Also, a few of those who have converted to Christianity from Islam have been imprisoned, and there is evidence that the government has been using the Maintenance of Internal Security Act to detain Christian workers involved in social action.

Bishops from Japan spoke of the difficulty of evangelizing in a secular, affluent society where people are very honest and have no obvious social needs. When Christianity came to Japan people were eager to be absorbed into Western culture. But now Christianity is regarded as foreign. But with Japan becoming an international secular society, what does becoming indigenous involve? Christians comprise 1 per cent of the population and the Anglican Church has 60,000 members. Christians are mostly from the middle and upper classes, well educated and affluent. One of the tasks of the Church is to raise the consciousness of the people of the country about the Two Thirds World.

In South Korea, the Protestant Churches are growing apace. Christianity is identified with Korean nationalism, since Christians were in the forefront of the resistance to Japanese religion during the Japanese occupation of Korea in the middle of the twentieth century. Evangelism is having a major impact among young conscripts to the army. Bishop Simon Sung Soo Kim of Seoul sees evangelism by Anglicans as more ecumenical than others, in not seeking to win members for their own Church; and in sending young clergy to live with the people wherever they are.

In Pakistan, the Church supported and made common cause with the women who were protesting against the oppression of President Zia's attempts to create an Islamic state. In India the issue of the Dalits and Harijans, the outcastes who form 20 per cent of the country's 800 million people, challenges the commitment of the Church to human liberation.

In Africa, religion is equally dominant. Though tribal religion is fast disappearing, the people are fundamentally religious. There is either wholesale conversion to Christianity, which leaves very little of the previous culture remaining, or it bows to the other Asian religion in Africa—Islam. Tribal religion is no real challenge to the propagation of the Christian faith. But as we shall see later, bishops from Nigeria and the Sudan spoke of real confrontation with Islam where any notion of dialogue is impossible.

Archbishop George Browne of Liberia saw the religious context as a positive advantage for evangelism in Africa: 'One of the advantages we have in evangelism in Africa is that the African is religious. His every movement is governed either by the Spirit or by the highest god, so wherever he goes, religion is there. So it is easy for us to pick up from there, like Paul or Barnabas, and say "this unknown God is the one I have brought". I have brought this unknown God not only with the pure gospel, but making life whole, and by whole we mean freedom, literacy, selfhood, health etc. Whether we like it or not, evangelism has to start first of all with the selfish part: where people are, where their needs are. After you get the individual, you can talk about the horizontal relationship. But we do not have much problem with the horizontal relationship because people accept that automatically. You do not need to sell that. What you need to sell, basically, is [the gospel] in the context of the African religion that feeds on fear. It is a religion of fear. "They are going to do this or that to me." "Everybody is out to get me." Christianity is a religion that demonstrates *love*. Now all you have to do is to try to get over the message, "from this thing you are fearing, we have a greater spirit who can liberate you". *That* is the selling point and if we can get that selling point over to him, that is when we will move more freely.'

In Latin America liberation theologians reflecting on the Marxist analysis of society have enabled the Church to relate to the injustices of the poor among whom have emerged base communities which create new forms of Church life. The problems of the debt crisis, the enormous gap between rich and poor in Brazil, the destruction of the jungles, the power of the drug barons, and the struggles of Central America, all challenge the power of the gospel to transform human life.

The dominant religious reality in Latin America is Roman Catholicism, sometimes interweaved with strong folk religion.

Many see the future of the Latin American Church to lie in the renewal of the Roman Catholic Church. Among tribal groups outside the mainstream of the lives of their nations, Anglicans have had a particular ministry in helping them maintain their tribal identity. The tribal religion has not proved a barrier to evangelism.

In the North and the West, there is uncertainty as to whether to describe societies as secular or post-secular. Whereas some would claim that all talk of God and faith is meaningless, others are impressed by the rise of new religious movements which focus on human potential. Emphasis is placed on experience, plurality and choice, and on developing the potential within persons. The notion of sin, and of any judgements about forces in society that are alienating, is rejected. The demonic is masked as an experimentation of the rich possibilities of the human spirit. The category of demonic is now filled by any attempt to undermine such experimentation.

In such diverse contexts, how do Anglicans evangelize?

What kind of evangelism is being done?

Archbishop Manasses Kuria told us that, a few days before he left Kenya for Lambeth, he had opened and closed a nine-day crusade in Nairobi led by Reinhard Bonnke, a leader in the charismatic movement. This had been in preparation for four years and was a venture involving many Protestant denominations. During the meetings, people were encouraged to come forward for healing, including childless married women seeking to bear children. President Arap Moi and some of his officials asked Archbishop Kuria to invite him to attend, and later opened up the state radio and television channels to broadcast the meetings.

Bishop Moses Tay from Singapore has a 'PhD' programme of prayer, healing and deliverance. He spoke of his own personal ministry of prayer for healing with a paralysed lady in hospital, who 'felt something like an electric current pass through her body' and who was subsequently healed, and baptized.

In Burma, the former archbishop used to take bands of young people on evangelistic treks through the countryside. In Nigeria, student evangelism has become the evangelistic arm of one whole diocese.

The diocese of Mount Kenya East has a variety of programmes

where evangelism and development go hand in hand. Among the nomadic Turkana and Samburu people in the desert area in the north of the diocese, people are turning to Christ in large numbers. Bishop David Gitari tells how after he noticed a derelict church in the district, the remnants of an earlier attempt at outreach, he posted a young Kikuyu clergyman to this area in 1980. This clergyman followed a strategy devised by Father Vincent Donovan.[2] Donovan had achieved an evangelistic breakthrough by preaching the gospel to communities rather than individuals. He invited whole *manyattas* (nomadic settlements) to declare their faith in Christ. The vicar presented the gospel to the Turkana community as a whole. He, and his successors, visited a *manyatta*, and took care to meet the people and learn their customs and social courtesies. At the end of the visit, the vicar would call a meeting and invite a respected elder to begin the proceedings with a traditional prayer. The vicar would then explain some aspect of the Christian message. He always began with common ground in traditional Turkana religion: for example, God as Creator and Sustainer. In later meetings, he would present Jesus as the Son of this God, who was born and lived on earth and became the Saviour. He would explain how sin arose and how Jesus could deliver people from sin.

The hearers always had plenty of questions: Who exactly was this Jesus? What did he look like? If he was the Son of God the Provider, how could he help them when they were suffering from sickness and the effects of drought? The vicar did his best to answer the questions, invited the elder to close with further prayer, and bid his hearers farewell.

After several months, some members of the *manyatta*—perhaps five out of a group of twenty adults—would be ready for baptism. Experience showed that soon after the initial baptisms of those who seemed most ready, other members of the *manyatta* would also come forward to declare their allegiance to Christ. In this way, whole *manyattas* would be added to the Church.

Several factors contribute to this growth. One was the humility of successive vicars in setting aside their own Kikuyu culture and presenting the gospel in terms meaningful to the Turkanas and Samburus. They were flexible in allowing converts to develop new forms of Christian prayer and worship in line with their own traditions, rather than insisting on prayer book worship. A third factor was the self-reliance and responsibility which the converts were expected to show from the first: as elders of the new congregations, and also in devising and implementing self-help projects—for example, constructing schools and starting adult-literacy programmes. Finally, there was the goodwill resulting from the diocese's practical care for the people whether Christian or not; especially during the disastrous drought of 1984 when food supplies and goats for restocking were distributed by the diocese.

In the longer first draft of his paper to the Conference, Bishop Gitari had written of the Church's work in this area: 'We proclaimed the gospel in its holistic richness. We carry out programmes for community health education and livestock development as well as feeding the hungry. We are also interested in issues of justice and peace as they arise. Hitherto the nomadic peoples of Northern Kenya had had little contact with the national and international structures which frequently oppress the poor and disadvantaged. However as Kenya develops, the long isolation of the North is coming to an end, and the nomadic peoples are increasingly coming into contact with powers which they cannot control.'

Proclaiming the gospel in Africa

The public call that Lambeth should call on all Anglicans to evangelize, was made by Bishop Dinis Sengulane of Lebombo, Mozambique, in the hour given to the African agenda. He spoke of evangelism most movingly to sustained applause.

Bishop Sengulane first argued that the Church exists to evangelize, and has good news which must be shared. He said: 'We would like the Lambeth Conference to call on all Anglicans to evangelize. The consequence of evangelism will be the increase of the number of people with whom we have spoken about Jesus Christ, and an increase in the number of places where Jesus Christ has been proclaimed. The only decisive reason why we evangelize is because Jesus founded the Church and ordered it to evangelize. The very name evangel means good news. All good news has to be shared with others. Any one who keeps quiet, however respectable he may look, has not had in his own heart any good news.'

Secondly, he pointed out that when the gospel is preached, people respond in a variety of different contexts. The Church is growing as a direct result of evangelism in Mozambique, Kenya, Burundi, Papua New Guinea, in the United States and South America. In Mozambique, a Marxist country, all church buildings have become too small for the numbers of people who have become Christians in recent times as a direct result of evangelism. In England, a priest told him that in one year, 300 young men became Christians as a result of evangelism. Such courageous and exciting results are a challenge to think of the many who are outside and to engage in further evangelism. Not everyone will respond positively to evangelism. But even a negative response may inspire others to follow a more positive response.

Thirdly, the gospel demands a personal and individual response. Many people have not heard the gospel as a personal message. They may have heard of and seen the Church, but not the challenging message that the promises of God are for them personally.

Fourthly, dialogue with other faiths is no substitute for evangelism. Bishop Sengulane continued: 'We have heard about Islamic growth through their proselytism and through the way they use money and donation of material things to gain a response to their claims. We know also of violence which they use. Dialogue is not a substitute for evangelism, and sensitivity is not a substitute for bold witness. The answer, as far as we Churches are concerned, is a bold evangelization, never allowing the uniqueness of Jesus Christ to be overshadowed by whatever pressures they may place. Lives and property have been lost among members of our Church because of the presence of Islamic fundamentalism. Mohammad may be a good prophet and a good person. But only Jesus Christ is the saviour of all and the prince of peace.'

He drew attention to a spectrum of ideologies, from doctrinaire Marxism to doctrinaire capitalism, flooding into countries in his continent. For him, sharing the gospel is the only answer to all ideologies. But he fails to recognize the possibility that the way the gospel is expressed, formulated and shared could itself be ideologically shaped.

He was acutely aware of the issues of hunger, poverty and violence in his continent. He does not see any real need for people to go hungry in the 1980s, or for violence—which is a sign of lack of mutual acceptance. Such matters called for an urgent need to evangelize so that people could become brothers and sisters in the Lord.

While he appears to have a single issue and to have only one agenda, he is strongly convinced that in the midst of all these issues, evangelism must have the central place. He does not present evangelism as the only answer, but as the central answer without which all the other answers are impotent.

The 'how' of evangelism

For Dinis Sengulane, the *how* of evangelism began with prayer. First, evangelism is shaped by prayer. Second, evangelism is a responsibility of every baptized member, so every member is to be trained. Third, he insists that concrete planning focused on unreached groups of people is needed. This must include lapsed and indifferent Christians in the dioceses. Planning must be specific with measurable goals, and be situated in realistic time frames. The bishops are called on to be the authoritative resources for such evangelism.

Dinis Sengulane described engaging in evangelism and respond-ing to the social needs of Africa as distinct activities. However, he lives in a desperate situation where the whole of life is a matter of crisis management. Responding to poverty requires emergency measures, to feed people because they are going to die; responding to people's spiritual need also requires emergency measures—to save people who are going to an eternity without Christ.

Responding to human need

For Bishop Henry Okullu from Kenya, the gospel is holistic. In a press conference on the African presentations, he identified human dignity and justice as important priorities for the Church's mission in Africa.

'Priorities must also be localized. Something that is a priority in Nigeria may not be a priority in Kent. The word priority on its own does not mean anything. The priority for us in Africa, without excluding other concerns, is human dignity, people's rights that we still seem to be violating in many ways. We are concerned with improving the standard of living of our people. The gospel concerns not only our spiritual conversion but also to a born again Christian it means all these other things. So we are convinced that the gospel must be presented in a holistic way so that it ministers to every aspect of the human person. This is a priority that we bring with us.'

In the African plenary, Bishop Okullu spelt out in detail the concern for justice in the African context.

He began with issues of repression of political dissent: 'About six million refugees in Africa have been forced out of their own motherlands. Political systems represented mainly by minority dictatorships and one party governments is the one major cause for the plight of these refugees now being looked after mainly by the Churches. The Churches are often asked to provide an ambulance service without asking about the cause of the casualties. African political leadership ruthlessly suppresses pluralism and totally rejects any alternative voice or power centre. This is the cause for endemic civil wars such as have been going on in Uganda for the last twenty years; for the persistent existence of repressive regimes such as in Zaire or Liberia. In Kenya for the last two years there has been a persistent debate between Church and state. Many Church leaders have been denounced and even been discussed in the national assembly.'

He pointed out that there was urban decay in Nairobi and Lagos; and violation of human rights in the Sudan where some parents in the south were selling their children into slavery instead of seeing them starve to death. In the face of these bitter realities, the Church is called to speak and act for justice, compassion, community, true peace and freedom, and the dignity of every person. Unless African governments become tolerant of dissenting voices, there will be no peaceful change of the government except through the military. Change there must always be.

He targeted the complicity of Western nations in the social problems of Africa: 'But your nations in the West cannot wholly be absolved from these political ills in Africa. Some of your nations support and sustain some of Africa's worst dictators by supplying them with guns to protect themselves from their fellow country-men. [Applause.] Why do your nations not supply us with food to feed our starving children in the sub-Sahara Africa instead of supplying us with guns to kill each other? Your governments subsidise your farmers to overproduce food, and that food is then thrown into the sea or fed to cattle while other human beings are starving to death elsewhere.

'The economic front is where we find injustices of the first order. Africa must sell to your countries cheaply and must buy dearly from them. Kenya produces one of the best coffees of the world but its price is set in New York, London or Paris. There is in your people a total lack of political will to create a new international economic order. On the international debt crisis, your nations have failed to honour the Lome agreement made between African, Caribbean and Pacific areas. We shall expect this Lambeth Conference not only to speak about rescheduling of the debt, but even recommending a complete cancelling of some of the crippling debts in sub-Saharan Africa. We shall expect the Churches in Africa to raise their voices strongly against the capital flight from some of our nations into Swiss banks. We shall need to speak to our African political leaders on the proper use of the borrowed funds. More often than not these funds only find themselves going into areas with a stronger political influence—developing mainly in tribal areas to which the heads of states belong.'

While Bishop Okullu fulminated against the forces beyond Africa's control that dominate and possibly bring to birth the variety of problems, he recognized that the answers must come from Africans themselves. While tribalism, corruption and other endemic problems of Africa construct self-erected barriers to development, he sets an agenda for the Churches to think, work hard and co-operate together to provide some answer to the seemingly intractable social problems of the continent.

Barriers to evangelism in Africa

Archbishop George Browne of Liberia also spoke of some aspects of African culture which were barriers to evangelism: 'Culture is judged by Scripture. Certain parts of a culture are hooked up with the religion of the people. Witchcraft, for example, is part of the culture and of the religion. So we have to dissociate what elements of the culture belong in the traditional religion and what elements just belong to the culture *per se*, and choose the one that is not in complete contradiction to Scripture. Hearing some of the speakers at Lambeth, I have begun to search in my mind as to whether the gospel imperative can be relative to culture.'

He told us that another obstacle for evangelism in African culture is polygamy, and consulting mediums in divination. When Christianity comes into African culture, it asks the individual to take a 180 degree turn. It is the only religion in the world that makes that demand of an individual. To ask people who have been used to concrete things they can see, such as medicine and many wives, to leave their home in faith as Abraham was requested to leave home and go to another land is not easy. Sometimes, when they join the Christian religion, they are disowned by the rest of the family. Archbishop Browne's grandfather was the custodian of the medicine for his village. And by tradition, his oldest son should have inherited this. Archbishop Browne is the oldest son of that oldest son, and was supposed to inherit that medicine bag for the town. But his mother's father was an Anglican priest. She did not want her child to be brought up as a heathen, so she stole him away from the village. It was a long time before they could recognize him as one of their sons. It was not until he was ordained to the priesthood that they accepted him. It is an expensive faith.

He continued: 'Sometimes when I am speaking to the people I say, "In me you not only have two ethnic groups crossing, you have two religions meeting. That is hope for you. I was where you sat. And if I could get on this side and still be alive and happy and active, why don't you come?" It makes it easier for me to get to that person, because I can say to them: "I know about medicine, what it does, and the reasons behind it. I want you to know that I was there. Today I am here. Let me tell you how I got here, and what I have taught on this side." This makes my ministry unique among my people.'

The most critical issue raised in evangelism in all the diverse contexts represented by the bishops, is the issue of gospel and culture. It was this that Lambeth focused on.

Gospel and culture

The setpiece plenary presentation on the Gospel and Culture proved to be an evening filled with passion. The plan of the evening announced by the chairman, Archbishop David Penman, was for each speaker to take twenty minutes to present his perspective. There would then be questions from the floor to the speakers and some interaction between them.

The first speaker was Bishop Bashir Jeevan from Hyderabad in Pakistan, resplendent in white robe and with a distinctive red cloth over one shoulder. He spoke passionately of the task of presenting the gospel in the context of other faiths. His conviction was that to start with theological and apologetic debate with non-Christians would not achieve anything. The focus must be on Jesus and on prayer: 'People want to hear about Jesus. Non-Christians want to be prayed for in the name of Jesus. They confess at the time of prayer that Jesus is able to heal them and bring them peace. Where there has been an awakening, people have been praying.'

He told us in an interview about his own experience of mission among the 3 million tribal Hindus who were in his diocese: 'I went into a village where all the Malwadi Bhils lived except one Midwar family whom I used to stay with, and talk and eat. The Bhils came to visit and listen, but would not take a cup of tea. I thought this was because the Midwar family was poor. I learned later it was because they were of low caste. After six months the village came to me to request baptism. They explained that they had been listening carefully to his conversations and believed Jesus was the only saviour. I baptized 130 people. At the end of the service, the headman got up and said: "Reverend, Redosee Midwar is of a lower caste. When you first came to our village and stayed with them, we were very much annoyed with you. Every time you left the village we all got together and discussed these things. There was hatred and opposition to you. But then some of us started thinking about you that as a Christian your way of thinking was altogether different. We thought the things you were saying were good; that you loved people and did not care about the caste system. Your lifestyle and words have convicted us of our hatred of the low caste people. Then we decided to get baptized."'

This story illustrates Bishop Jeevan's approach of positive presentation, and his conviction about the work of the Holy Spirit in people's lives. He found it difficult to evangelize Muslims, because Christians are identified with Western nations who have not treated the Muslims well politically speaking. A further hindrance in his view was 'disbelief in the bodily resurrection of Jesus Christ and the claim that it was only a spiritual experience of resurrection in the minds of the disciples.' He argued that such theological controversies damaged the missionary and evangelistic tasks in Asia, since Muslims then felt that they believed more about the uniqueness of Christ than Christians who did not believe in the resurrection of Christ or the authority of the Bible.

This was a clear reference to the speaker due to follow him, David Jenkins of Durham. Bishop Jeevan had spoken with fervour for over twice his allotted time. There was some movement on the platform as David Jenkins told David Penman that since Bishop Jeevan had taken up his own time as well, the third speaker, Bishop David Gitari, should speak. But David Gitari says: 'I told Bishop Jenkins that many people had come to hear him. I also felt that he needed to have the opportunity to defend himself against Bishop Jeevan's implication that he did not believe in the resurrection.'

Evangelism in secular society

For Bishop Jenkins, the context of evangelism was the secular culture of England, which, in Mediterranean and medieval Christian terms was considered a Christian country. Despite a great deal of publicly expressed nostalgia about being basically a Christian country, in descriptive, quantitative and New Testament terms it was plainly not.

'In the post-Christendom and post-Christian culture of Britain, with all its pluralisms of religions, secularities of approach and uncertain clamour of voices on all matters of values, politics and practices . . . the central gospel issue is that of the true and living God against all idolatries, atheisms and indifferences.' In such a context, it was difficult to identify what shape the gospel really takes.

In such a situation, Bishop Jenkins claimed that 'primary evangelization'—in the sense of preaching the gospel, and receiving a positive response by which people are recruited to membership of the body of Christian believers who had not been members before—did not work. In England and Durham it was not all that frequent or widespread, did not have much of an impact on the country or on the growth of the Church, and was not regarded as the right or feasible way of witnessing to the gospel because the majority of parishes did not practise it.

He questioned whether this was the pattern for today, because life for the Church has become immensely complicated since the original primary evangelism of the first chapters of Acts. Firstly, the 'coming wrath' had not yet arrived, in the decisive and final sense in which the New Testament clearly expected that the final End would arrive—either in, or very soon after, the lifetimes of some of the first generation of disciples.

David Jenkins continued: 'Secondly, the early Church soon began to reckon with an extension of the time available to them and to the world as part of the mercy of God. Time was to be given to preach the gospel to all nations and the End was to be delayed until this could be completed.

'Thirdly, the notion of the selected few called out of every nation to be able to survive through wrath through baptism in Jesus and to live with God in the eternity of his Kingdom became seriously obscured and considerably altered in its whole dynamic and meaning when Christianity received its Constantinian establishment. Now Christianity was the religion of society as such and "the Wrath" soon developed into the Final Judgement which each individual soul would have to face, rather than the imminent "End" of the world. So the way was open to the individualizing of the whole notion of salvation and to the medieval pictures of Death, Judgement, Heaven and Hell. Fourthly, evangelization became the thrust to "christianize" Europe, i.e. to spread Christian civilization—and this spilled over, when the Europe of medieval Christendom was already breaking up, in to missionary attempts to christianize what, for Mediterranean and European-centred Christians, was "overseas". All this meant that European imperial expansion and Christian missionary expansion and European civilization expansion became inextricably mixed up.

'Where does this leave us in a world-wide gathering like this, a world-wide gathering which is much shaped by English imperialism, even if it is not determined by it any more nor all that identified with that particular feature of nearly past history? And where does that leave us with regard to evangelization in England itself? . . . What of primary evangelization now?

'Any answers to these questions, surely, depend on how the contemporary Christian Church understands that continuing enterprise of God to which the Christian Church and the Christian enterprise are supposed to be essentially linked. The uncertainties and differences which we have here in England and in the Diocese of Durham about primary evangelization reflect the uncertainties and differences among us about the central and simple understanding of the nature of God's enterprise to which Jesus Christ is the central clue and the defining Word.

'The central issue which provides the practical base for, and points to the practical direction of, primary evangelization is "who do we believe God to be and what do we believe God to be doing?" The central issue and content of the gospel is not Jesus but God.

'On the one hand, to preach and practise a "churchly" gospel which endeavours to recruit people into a cultic community which is aligned chiefly on their individual salvation and their pastoral care is simply to deny, or at any rate devastatingly to diminish, the actual and realistic claims for the gospel of the New Testament. The gospel is plainly about the true and living God of all peoples in the total universe who is at work to fulfil that Kingdom which is the completion of his purposes of holiness, righteousness and love which were expressed in creation, pursued in redemption and promised in judgement and completion.'

When we discussed the implications of Bishop Jenkins's speech with him, we asked what the basis was for calling someone to the Way if we had no belief in something of great and true value now. He replied: 'There is something of truth and value now, and that is precisely why I am obliged on what has been given me through the biblical tradition through my membership of the Church. It is precisely on the basis of having been given that faith and commitment and a call that I raise these questions.'

Incarnational evangelism in Kenya

David Gitari presented a model of incarnational evangelism. He took the gospel as given, but also worked out carefully how he applied it in his culture. For him, culture included customs, focusing especially on the custom of polygamy and the communal nature of living in society. The concept of persons in community is fundamental to evangelism, and to an integral link between evangelism and social action. The Great Commission and the Great Commandment belong together.

The gospel and traditional customs

He identified as a major problem the need to remove the Western cultural wrapper and to let the gospel encounter African cultures directly. A useful distinction about the customs of those to whom the gospel is brought, is that some customs the gospel cannot tolerate—for example twin-destruction, witchcraft, sorcery and cattle-rustling. Some can be tolerated for the time being—for example, the circumcision of women and polygamy. Other customs are fully acceptable to the gospel—for example, many customs associated with marriage, African hospitality, and the community's relation to the individual.

David Gitari said: 'We are not sentimental admirers of traditional cultures. Sometimes, the gospel frankly opposes the cherished beliefs of a people. The Masai believe that all the cattle in the world belong to them, and that any cattle currently being kept by other tribes are in the wrong hands and may be retrieved by the Masai. Jesus, the judge of culture, must visit the Masai and tell them, "If you love your neighbouring tribe, the WaKamba, do not steal their cattle."'

Bishop Gitari argued that godly discernment was needed to determine which customs, though not ideally Christian, are nevertheless tolerable to the gospel by the criteria that there is no clear teaching against them in the Scriptures, and that they are likely to die a natural death when the Christian Church is firmly established. There was one case of great importance for Africa when the Anglican Church failed to recognize a tolerable custom. The year 1988 marked the centenary of the Lambeth Conference's decisive, and he believed mistaken, refusal of baptism to polygamists.

'The issue of polygamy', Bishop Gitari continued, 'meets our suggested criteria: the New Testament contains no implicit or explicit statement on polygamy, unless it is Paul's instruction that bishops and deacons should be married to only one wife (1 Tim. 3. 2,12). However, polygamist men who want to become Christians have been handled as if their condition were intolerable to the gospel. The 1888 Lambeth Conference (attended by about 104 bishops, of whom Crowther of Niger was the only black bishop present) resolved that persons living in polygamy be not admitted to baptism.'

The consequences for mission of Lambeth 1888's decision were plain. The chief of a large tribe in West Africa heard the gospel from missionaries and expressed the desire to be baptized. But he was given the condition that he must send away all but one of his wives. The good news became bad news, and he expelled the missionaries. A few months later Muslim missionaries arrived and told the chief that he could become a Muslim and keep his wives. He and his entire tribe embraced Islam.

David Gitari went on: 'The Church in Africa should approach polygamists with greater pastoral sensitivity. In the new Canon on Marriage in the Church of the Province of Kenya, those who were polygamists before they were Christians are tolerated. When they accept the gospel they are baptized, together with their believing wives and children, without making any condition of sending away their wives. The expelling of such wives is a worse evil than keeping them. I would have wished this Lambeth Conference to review the decision made by our predecessors at Lambeth in 1888.'

Winning communities to Christ

Bishop Gitari continued: 'Yet the gospel is also the preserver of culture, cherishing some parts of African culture and transforming them for the service of Christ. One of the most important aspects of African culture which the gospel affirms is the African understanding of humanity. Although an individual has his own unique personality, Dr John Mbiti is right to say that in African thought the individual is fully a person only in the context of the community. The individual can only say "I am, because we are; and since we are, therefore I am."

Bishop Gitari argued that the African Church has inherited from the Western Church a concept of evangelism as winning individuals to Jesus Christ. Each person has individually to accept Christ as a personal saviour. But the concept of an individual making a major decision in his life alone is alien to African culture. When a young person wishes to get married, the decision is so important that the whole family, and indeed the entire clan, has to be involved. Making a decision to follow Christ could also be said to be so important that it should not be left to an individual.

David Gitari continued: 'We are convinced that our approach should not be that of rescuing individuals from a sinking boat but rather winning communities to Jesus Christ. We are not evangelizing individuals to pluck them out of their communities; but after a period of instruction, communities are turning to Christ and being baptized, and are being incorporated into the life of a community based Church.'

Evangelism and social responsibility

Bishop Gitari declared: 'There is no question of regarding evangelism as primary and seeing our social responsibility as secondary in our mission to the people of Northern Kenya. These nomadic peoples are faced with the implications of climatic change which has resulted in a series of disastrous droughts in recent years. We have a saying that "a hungry stomach has no ears". We cannot preach first and then feed people afterwards. We have refused to put a wedge between evangelism and socio-political responsibility. We believe that this approach is required by obedience to the Great Commission and the Great Commandment.

'Naturally it is vital that our social activity is carried out in an appropriate manner, just as much as our evangelism. If our efforts to help the poor make them dependent on us, then we have not liberated them.

'Evangelism is the proclamation of the historical biblical Christ as Saviour and Lord with a view to persuading people to turn to him and be reconciled with him. Models of evangelism are many, but I have attempted to share with you a model which could be described as "Incarnational" based on the perception that Jesus "emptied himself" and chose to "become flesh" and "to live among us". By entering on the stage of human history he was able to identify himself with humanity and to reveal God and to serve mankind. The Incarnational Model demands our Christian presence in the world so that we may be able to share Jesus Christ with the communities and people we encounter. The Incarnational Model also invites us to proclaim the gospel not from a distance but rather by penetrating into communities and cultures whose customs are either endorsed, challenged or transformed by the gospel. In this way, we believe we are obeying the Great Commission and as a result "The Lord is adding to our numbers those who are being saved".

Bishop Gitari's call for a change in the stance on polygamy caused immense interest in Kenya. We shall discuss that in the next chapter where we examine the Conference and the media.

Assessment

How should the discussion on evangelism and mission at Lambeth be evaluated? It has to be said that the plenary presentations and their associated stories made for a very thin foundation on which to commit the whole communion to a decade of evangelism. The issue of the relation of the gospel and culture was never really discussed. The issue of sin never really emerged. How is sin identified and addressed in cultures? If sin is removed, the understanding of grace becomes distorted. How can grace be understood when sin is not clearly understood? There was no interaction between the various views of evangelism which were represented by the bishops. In calling for a decade of evangelism, what understanding of evangelism had the bishops called the communion to? To confront the Muslims? A power encounter against occult powers? To confront the Western powers that support dictators? To evangelize all but the Jews (as we shall see in the next chapter)? To abandon primary evangelization as unworkable in secular contexts? The African bishops whom we have quoted knew the basis on which they evangelized. But such a basis was not articulated or discussed.

There is a grave danger that with this decade of evangelism, any activity that seeks to reach out to others will be justified in the name of evangelism. We need to identify the common elements in the presentations as well as in the convictions shared by the bishops. Can any agreed elements be discerned? First, there is an agreement on the givenness of the gospel. Bishops Jeevan, Jenkins and Gitari represented three approaches to evangelism. Bishop Jeevan held that the same words and formulations of the gospel that have always been used, still work. He concluded therefore that the gospel is true and must be true for every situation. His experience is authentic, but are his conclusions acceptable?

For Bishop Gitari, the gospel is given from the scriptural revelation. But the formularies in which it was given are not those in which it is necessarily to be applied. The local culture plays an important part in how the evangelizing Church shapes its presentation, and how the people being evangelized receive it.

Bishop Jenkins affirmed in his presentation, and in conversation with us, his commitment to the given gospel of God. The question he would pose to Bishop Jeevan is whether the gospel he shares is really the gospel, or whether it is just a tradition because the issue of gospel and culture had not been examined adequately. The given was accepted as it was and applied. If it worked it was authenticated. But Jenkins firmly asserted that it did not work in his situation.

With Bishop Gitari, he took a different approach. In the press conference after their presentations, Jenkins turned to Gitari and said, 'I need to learn from you.' What did he mean? The issue for Jenkins was, How does what we know as the gospel become good news for people today? He resists the view that because the gospel works in one situation it must be good news as it stands applied in the same way in every situation. In Bishop Gitari, he perhaps saw someone who had taken the given gospel, applied it creatively and found it to work. For it seemed that Bishop Jenkins recognized in Bishop Gitari's example a contemporary situation where the gospel was at work. Bishop Jenkins could not say the same about his hard situation in England with David Gitari's degree of confidence and certainty, but he was open to examining a situation from outside his context and learning from it.

This recognition is a sign of the emergence of unity. For the Two Thirds World Churches and Churches in the West have a lot to learn from each other about evangelism. There is the need to strengthen the ties in the communion that enable theology done in the context of the life of communities to be shared widely, and to encourage this kind of theological activity in the West in the older churches, where the dominant form of theology has been from a speculative point of view. It is quite possible for there to be an intuitive perception of issues and for people to arrive at conclusions and faith commitments which may go beyond conceptualising.

It is clear from the Lambeth experience that there is a desperate need for this kind of theology done in communities of people responding to the realities of their own situation to be shared between various contexts to a far greater extent before people are able to make final statements.

Intra-contextual sharing

As Bishops Gitari and Jeevan enter into the struggles of David Jenkins in his concern to make the gospel relevant in his own context, they will begin to discover those areas where at present they are *not* able to make the gospel relevant in their contexts. For while Bishops Gitari and Jeevan may be successful in some areas, they are not successful in all. There may be subcultures in their society that have proved resistant to the gospel. And Bishop Jenkins found it hard to identify any area where he could point to success. This is where the experience of South Asia could have assisted. Bishop Jeevan would know people who represented very secular views; the educated elite of those cities who, though they have a veneer of religious adherence, are very secular in their approach to life. Will the gospel work apart from converting a few individuals? Will it make sense to the majority of such a group? The South Asian context, with its variety of cultures of great affluence and intellect, and its business communities, is a great resource if the Church will examine and approach it with humility.

This is the main point of the Lambeth Conference. What is the meaning of Christian communion if one part of the world can theologize in its own context without taking into consideration the experiences of other parts of the world before making statements? The need for mutual accountability is the theological basis for communion.

Convergence

In the presentations and concerns of Bishops Gitari and Okullu, we saw an expression of a growing convergence on mission and evangelism in the Two Thirds World. Both are senior office-holders in the World Council of Churches. Both spoke of the necessity and reality of personal conversion and social transformation.

A number of international statements on mission and evangelism in the last ten years have described mission and evangelism in similar terms. *The Lausanne Covenant* was produced in 1974. Bishop David Gitari is a member of the Lausanne Committee for World Evangelization, to which the covenant gave birth. On evangelism and Christian social responsibility it said: 'Evangelism itself is the proclamation of the historical, biblical Christ as Saviour and Lord, with a view to persuading people to come to him personally and so be reconciled to God. The results of evangelism include obedience to Christ, incorporation into his

Church and responsible service in the world [paragraph 4]. We affirm that God is both the Creator and the Judge of all men. We therefore should share his concern for justice and reconciliation throughout human society and for the liberation of men from every kind of oppression. Although reconciliation with man is not reconciliation with God, nor is social action evangelism, nor is political liberation salvation, nevertheless we affirm that evangelism and socio-political involvement are both part of our Christian duty. For both are necessary expressions of our doctrines of God and man, our love for our neighbour and our obedience to Jesus Christ. The message of salvation implies also a message of judgement upon every form of alienation, oppression and discrimination and we should not be afraid to denounce evil and injustice wherever they exist. When people receive Christ they are born again into his kingdom and must seek not only to exhibit but also to spread its righteousness in the midst of an unrighteous world. The salvation we claim should be transforming us in the totality of our personal and social responsibilites. Faith without works is dead' [paragraph 5].[3]

Bishop Gitari is also vice-moderator of the Commission for World Mission and Evangelism of the World Council of Churches. This body produced the statement in 1982 entitled 'Mission and Evangelism—An Ecumenical Affirmation' which said: 'The Church is sent into the world to call people and nations to repentance, to announce forgiveness of sin and a new beginning in relation with God and with neighbours through Jesus Christ.' [Preface]. 'At the very heart of the Church's vocation in the world is the proclamation of the kingdom of God inaugurated in Jesus the Lord, crucified and risen. Through its internal life of Eucharistic worship, through planning for mission and evangelism, through a daily life-style of solidarity with the poor, through advocacy even to confrontation with the powers that oppress human beings, the Churches are trying to fulfil this evangelistic vocation. [paragraph 6]

'The starting point of our proclamation is Christ and Christ crucified. "We preach Christ crucified, a stumbling block to Jews and folly to Gentiles" (1 Cor.1.23). The Good News handed on to the Church is that God's grace was in Jesus Christ, who "though he was rich, yet for your sake he became poor, so that by his poverty you might become rich" (2 Cor. 8:9) [paragraph 7].

'The proclamation of the gospel includes an invitation to recognize and accept in a personal decision the saving Lordship of Christ. It is the announcement of a personal encounter, mediated by the Holy Spirit, with the living Christ, receiving his forgiveness and making a personal acceptance of the call to discipleship and a new life of service. God addresses himself specifically to each of his children, as well as to the whole human race. Each person is entitled to hear the good news. Many social forces today press for conformity and passivity. Masses of poor people have been deprived of their right to decide about their lives and the life of their society. While anonymity and marginalization seem to reduce the possibilities for personal decisions to a minimum, God as Father knows each one of his children and calls each of them to make a fundamental personal act of allegiance to him and his kingdom in the fellowship of his people' [paragraph 10].

'The call to conversion, as a call to repentance and obedience, should also be addressed to nations, groups and families. To proclaim the need to change from war to peace, from injustice to justice, from racism to solidarity, from hate to life is a witness rendered to Jesus Christ and to his kingdom. The prophets of the Old Testament addressed themselves constantly to the collective conscience of the people of Israel calling the rulers and the people to repentance and to renewal of the covenant' [paragraph 12].

'In the fulfilment of its vocation, the Church is called to announce Good News in Jesus Christ, forgiveness, hope, a new heaven and a new earth, to denounce powers and principalities, sin and injustice; to console the widows and orphans, healing, restoring the brokenhearted; and to celebrate life in the midst of death. In carrying out these tasks, Churches may meet limitations, constraints, even persecution from prevailing powers which pretend to have final authority over the life and destiny of people' [paragraph 16].[4]

In 1983, an international conference of theologians and practitioners of development affirmed in 'Transformation—The Church in Response to Human Need'[5]: 'According to the biblical view of human life, then, transformation is the change from a condition of human existence contrary to God's purposes to one in which people are able to enjoy fullness of life in harmony with God (John 10.10; Col. 3. 8-15; Eph. 4.13). This transformation can only take place through the obedience of individuals and communities to the gospel of Jesus Christ, whose power changes the lives of men and women by releasing them from the guilt, power and consequences of sin, enabling them to respond with love toward God and toward others (Rom. 5.5), and making them "new creatures in Christ" (2 Cor. 5.17).'

'There are a number of themes in the Bible which help us to focus on the way we understand transformation. The doctrine of creation speaks of the worth of every man, woman and child, of the responsibility of human beings to look after the resources of nature (Gen 1.26-30) and to share them equitably with their neighbours. The doctrine of the Fall highlights the innate tendency of human beings to serve their own interests, with the consequences of greed, insecurity and the lust for power. "God's judgement rightly falls upon those who do such things" (Rom. 2.2). The doctrine of redemption proclaims God's forgiveness of sins and the freedom Christ gives for a way of life dedicated to serving others by telling them about the Good News of Salvation, bringing reconciliation between enemies, and losing one's life to see justice established for all exploited people' [paragraphs 11 and 12].

The theme of transformation, and strong echoes of other sections of this statement, appear in the report of the Mission and Ministry section of the Conference.

A fourth statement was prepared by a consultation of the Commission for World Mission and Evangelism of the World Council of Churches in Stuttgart in 1987.[6] It affirmed that: 'the essence of this Good News is that God was in Christ reconciling the world unto himself and has now called us to a ministry of reconciliation. This ministry pertains both to reconciliation between God and humans, as well as to reconciliation between individuals and groups alienated from each other. The gospel is the good news of the possibility of a new beginning. This ministry of reconciliation has, however, to be exercised within the specific context of every person and every group. There are different entry points for the love of God into the lives of people, both as individuals and as communities. It is only in dependence upon God's Spirit that we can develop a sensitivity toward these and thus become able to minister authentically to people's deepest needs.

'The Church's evangelistic ministry can never be detached from its other ministries. If the Church chooses to remain silent in the face of injustice and oppression, both in society at large and in the Church itself, it jeopardizes its entire evangelistic ministry. These concerns—which Scripture consistently summarizes as the plight of the widow, the orphan, the alien and the poor—are inseparably related to evangelism and every effort to drive a wedge between these is to be rejected as the proclamation of a spurious gospel.

'In our evangelism we are challenged to be sensitive to people's cultures. This means, *inter alia*, that we cannot simply export models of evangelism from one culture to another. Some of us are particularly concerned about the highly individualistic approach in evangelism in the West which is often conducted in exactly the same way in other parts of the world, with the result that converts are often isolated and even alienated from their families and communities. We were reminded of the fact that, in some cultures, important decisions—and is not the decision to become a disciple of Jesus Christ an eminently important one?—are never taken individually but always corporately. We must respect such values in these cultures, not least because they help us become more sensitive to the biblical understanding of our humanity, and also challenge the excessive individualism in some cultures' [paragraphs 1, 2, 6 and 10].

These statements, drawn up by international consultations, represent the mission understanding of large sections of the Church in the Two Thirds World. Thus these African bishops, in affirming their commitment to evangelism and mission to the whole person and whole society, are working and speaking from a well-articulated theological basis.

People not structures

All the presentations made at Lambeth focused on people. In some World Council of Churches circles there has been a concentration on evangelizing the structures. This has often prevented Churches and people from actually proclaiming the gospel. It was therefore notable that at Lambeth, where many of the bishops had senior roles in the World Council, such language was absent. Certainly evangelism with the poor must be done in such a way that it witnesses to the gospel in relation to the structures. Bishop Okullu made that very clear. The people who experience the gospel are energized to address the structures and to relate more effectively to the process of dealing with systems and structures. Evangelism must be done in such a way that instead of being victims of the structures people are able to address the structures as the people of God. This is the priority of the gospel in any situation. The good news is that God accepts a person in Jesus Christ. To make that good news a priority requires an understanding of sin and of grace. These have to be at the beginning of anybody's experience of themselves as human beings. Human potential cannot begin to flower without the recognition of sin and the experience of grace. That is what the gospel is all about.

What the African bishops were articulating was that Jesus, God and the gospel are at the heart of evangelism. Dinis Sengulane's distinct activities of evangelism and responding to Africa's physical hunger both had the love of God at their heart. The African presentations affirmed that evangelism must take place in conjunction both with worship and with mission to the whole person and the whole society. The international debate shows that this is not a naive repetition of a gospel that no longer works in secular societies, but a carefully thought out theology and practice of holistic mission. Some such careful thought is desperately needed in the Anglican Communion as it begins its decade of evangelism lest, for lack of it, too many people conclude that it does not work.

Notes

1. Resolution 43.
2. Vincent Donovan, *Christianity Rediscovered* (London, SCM 1982).
3. *The Lausanne Covenant* (Lausanne Occasional Papers no.1, 1974).
4. 'Mission and Evangelism—an Ecumenical Affirmation' (*International Review of Mission*, Vol. LXXI no. 284 October 1982) pp. 427–451.
5. 'Transformation—The Church in Response to Human Need', in *The Church in Response to Human Need*, ed. by Vinay Samuel and Chris Sugden (Grand Rapids, Eerdmans, 1987) pp. 254 ff.
6. 'The Stuttgart Statement', (*A Monthly Letter on Evangelism*), no. 10/11, October/November 1987) (World Council of Churches), and in *Proclaiming Christ in Christ's Ways*, ed. by Vinay Samuel and Albrecht Hauser (Oxford, Regnum Books, 1989). The latter also contains the full text of David Gitari's presentation on 'Evangelization and Culture'.

CHAPTER 5

The Gospel amid Other Faiths

A second important issue identified in mission and evangelism was the relation between the gospel and other faiths. The struggles of the Christian Church in the context of Islam was most powerfully brought to the Conference's attention by the bishops from the Sudan and Nigeria. For them, the burning issue was the response of a minority Church to an aggressive Islam.

The presentation of the African bishops focuses as a priority concern the situation of Christianity in lands where Islamic fundamentalism is rampant. Bishop Daniel Zindo of Yambio, from the Episcopal Church of the Sudan, pointed out that Sudan was the largest country in Africa, and a most religious country where Islam is the faith of the majority. Christians comprise some 20 per cent of the total population, and there are also the African traditional religions.

Bishop Zindo told how the introduction of Shariah (the technical term for the law of Islam, the path to be followed by every Muslim), by the former president in 1982, had created a form of racism. The current president had left the country. Shariah law is to be reintroduced. Masses of Sudanese people, including Christians, have appealed to the government to remove the law, but all in vain. He understood that the new government, which includes the leader of the Islamic fundamentalists, was to make Shariah law effective within two months. At the time of Lambeth, only one month was left. It was still the cry of most people in the Sudan that the government should replace the Shariah with a form of law which punishes an offender and leaves room for repentance and reform. The Sudan Council of Churches, which includes all the other denominations, had made a protest to the government that was being considered.

He told how the five-year civil war had caused great loss of life and asked for Lambeth's help in persuading his government to bring peace. In 1986 the Christian Church in the Sudan was concerned about the suffering of the people and decided to ask if the Roman Catholic and Anglican archbishops could meet the president, the prime minister and also the leader of the Movement in the hope that peace could be brought to the country. There was no answer to that appeal. So Bishop Zindo appealed to the Anglican Communion as a whole to support the United Churches in the Sudan in their request to the government to discuss the problem and to change the law so that the people of the Sudan might be safe.

The Bishop of Kaduna, in Nigeria, spoke also on Islamic fundamentalism: 'if you heard of churches being burnt in March 1987, I was the principal person being attacked. It was in my diocese that churches were razed to the ground. Christians lost all their properties, not because they stole. We lost all our belongings because we proclaimed the name of Jesus Christ. That is why I am qualified to stand before you this afternoon.

'We have the traditionalist Muslims who accept things. But we have the militant ones who believe everything must be done by force. If you are not prepared to listen to them, you die. If you have a son who becomes a Christian, you are bound to kill that child. You have the authority to kill that child, and no court will question you as to why you destroyed your son. You cannot negotiate with someone who is not prepared to listen to or hear you, or even recognize you as a human being.

'You may possibly have heard after the March destruction that one of the leaders of Nigeria went on air to say that if after the democratically conducted elections, Muslims were not allowed to rule, the country should be divided. There was then an election at Ahmadu Bello University within our diocese and the Christians won. The Muslims went on a riot and implicated some Christians. This was when that university was closed down. It was as violent as that.

'When you apply for your own rights, you apply for a certificate of occupancy and present your money. The bishop before me applied in 1974 for a plot of land. They replied in 1978 to say that that application was receiving attention. Some land was taken away from us in 1963. They said, "do not worry bishop, we are going to give you some other land". That land has yet to be given. These are some of the things we go through.

'All our countries, including Great Britain, are being funded by Muslims. As Anglicans, Canterbury is our centre, London is our Medina. But no Christian is allowed to enter Mecca. But here you are giving them the opportunity not only to enter. But the Bishop of London very kindly said that we should now give them special time for devotion, which they would not do for us where I come from. I am not against that at all. But what I would like Islamists to do is, what we do for you here, do for us in your place.'

Loud applause followed.

Mission in the context of Islam and Judaism

Bishop Samir Kaffity described to us the practice of mission by Christians in the Middle East: 'Mission in my area is defined as love and service. It is not proclamation in the sense of proclaiming orally or in writing the word of God. It is living the word of God, being present as the living word of God among people, exactly as our Lord himself was in the Middle East. His ministry was more of service than proclamation. Four-fifths of our Lord's time was with the people in their problems and one-fifth was in the teaching ministry. We are engaged in service. The diocese has 32 institutions of service, more than the number of parishes. This was more a matter of choice than force of circumstances. We feel Christ can be communicated in an inter-religious situation when Christ is shown as the Good Samaritan, as the one who loves for love's sake, not for conversion's sake.

'We are either in theocratic or semi-religious states. The state of Israel passed an anti-mission law in 1977 against enticing people to join your persuasion. If you are found, you are subject to a penalty. In Muslim countries, it is very difficult to convert. However, in some of these countries there is freedom to change from one religion to another. We have different situations in the Middle East. However, no one can say no to a person who out of conviction and persuasion would like to join this or that religion or denomination. The first bishop was a convert from Judaism, a rabbi. We have had a priest who was a convert from Islam. He was killed by a bullet in 1948 during the clashes between both parties in Palestine. So we have also some converts in the diocese of Jerusalem. In sister dioceses there are converts from various religions, from Zoroastrianism, Judaism, Islam and others.'

The report and resolutions on inter-faith dialogue

The story of the Conference's handling of the issue of other faiths will need some time to elapse before it can be fully told. Those living in the Middle East saw the process of producing a report as subject to heavy pressure from a Jewish lobby trying to get the Lambeth Conference to change the Anglican stance on relations with Jews.

This suspicion appears to have some substance in the light of the following circumstances. The report on other faiths began as a report on Christian witness to Jews, prepared by Bishop Richard Harries of Oxford. It was pointed out at the press conference that the original press briefing at Lambeth Palace from the Archbishop of Canterbury before the Conference had indicated that the document would be mainly on Christians and Jews. The explanation given for finally focussing on Jews and Muslims was that it would have appeared 'very lopsided if Lambeth had simply produced a set of guidelines on Jewish-Christian relations and none on Christian-Muslim or Christian-Hindu relations. The state of the guidelines on Jewish-Christian relations were much further advanced than the other guidelines.' Yet people whose expertise was in the realm of Christian-Muslim relations were unhappy with accepting the document as it stood.

The original resolution before the Conference was: 'This Conference commends the document *Jews,Christians and Muslims: The Way of Dialogue* for study and encourages the Churches of the Anglican Communion to engage in dialogue with Jews and Muslims on this basis.' Archbishop David Penman pointed out that: 'we received this document only yesterday from the dogmatic and pastoral section. This may be the only place in this whole Conference where the Conference is being asked to commend action on a significant section paper being brought before the Conference at very short notice, without translation, and I suspect without the opportunity for many of us to read it. Many of us feel it is too early to accord the document a special status before it is carefully considered by certain of the Churches that it significantly affects and before it is properly translated and understood.'

The significance of this point is that the material on Muslims appears to have been a latecomer to a document whose original prime focus was on Jewish-Christian relationships and not to have been adequately examined by Christians in the areas where Christian-Muslim relations were paramount. Could not the lopsidedness of the document have been perceived earlier? It seems a weak explanation for the obviously hurried change in focus made during the Conference.

This report went through a number of drafts at the Conference. It was widened to cover witness among Muslims as well. The Council of Christians and Jews invited many Lambeth bishops out to dinner immediately prior to the evening's debate on the report. The reporter from the *New York Times* (where there is a large Jewish population) attended during the debate on other faiths, and his questions at the press conference showed especial interest in the earlier versions of the report (which only discussed relations with Jews). He also had to change his news story when Archbishop Penman successfully persuaded the Conference to note, rather than adopt, the report. Some even spoke privately of persistent lobbying by Jewish leaders.

There was clearly an issue at stake in the relations with Jews. At the press conference, where more points of substance seem to have been raised on this matter than in the plenary debate, the question was raised whether the Conference was being asked to take a view on the matter of conversion of Jews. Bishop Harries drew attention to the content of paragraph 26 of the document: 'there are a variety of attitudes towards Judaism within Christianity today. At one pole, there are those Christians whose prayer is that Jews, without giving up their Jewishness, will find their fulfilment in Jesus the Messiah. Indeed some regard it as their particular vocation and responsibility to share their faith with Jews, whilst at the same time urging them to discover the spiritual riches which God has given them through the Jewish faith. Other Christians, however, believe that in fulfilling the law and the prophets, Jesus validated the Jewish relationship with God, while opening this way up for Gentiles through his own person. For others, the holocaust has changed their perception, so that until Christian lives bear a truer witness, they feel a divine obligation to affirm the Jews in their worship and sense of the God and Father of Jesus. All these approaches recognize that Christians today are being called into a fresh, more fruitful relationship with Judaism. We urge that further thought and prayer, in the light of Scripture and the facts of history, be given to the nature of this relationship.'

Some were uneasy with this attempt to be even-handed. Bishop Derek Rawcliffe of Glasgow and Galloway, Scotland, called on the Conference to repudiate all persecution of Jews by Christians, to confess Christian involvement at various levels in such persecution in the past and present; to express corporate repentance for all such persecution; and to make an official statement of this repudiation, confession and repentance with the determination to do all in its power to prevent any continuance of persecution in any form. He hoped that the Conference would do this in earnest of good faith. But this did not imply that Christians accepted everything the State of Israel has done or is doing.

He continued: 'Neither does such an act of repentance mean, while we as Christians recognize with gratitude the roots from which we have come, we should cease to wish that Jews should wish to come to acceptance of Messiah Jesus as saviour, and to faith in him and the new life he offers. While I recognize what the document says about the way Judaism has developed from New Testament times until now, essential differences between our two faiths stem from our attitude to the Lord Jesus and his teaching. This has been borne in on me in the last year when I have heard Jews defining themselves in their own terms. I remember a programme on television in November 1987 about the holocaust. A rabbi was interviewed and, after describing his experiences in the concentration camps, he was asked by the interviewer: "Can you forgive those who did that to you?" He said, "No I can't forgive them; only God can forgive sins." And I thought, where did I hear that before?

'On another radio programme, another Jew was asked the same sort of question and said, "It is Christianity to forgive—the Jews want justice." It was in connection with trials of alleged war criminals. It is important to remember this and not equate the two faiths in some sort of wishy-washy way.

'We believe as Christians that all people in the world can look to Jesus and be saved; not that salvation is for certain nations and not for others. It is also for the Jews. In our dialogues and attempts to reach a more informed understanding of Judaism, we must not sell them short on what Jesus Christ has done for us. May I ask for that act of repentance and an understanding of what our Lord Jesus Christ calls us to do for the Jews as for all other peoples.'

Bishop Michael Nuttall of Natal, Southern Africa, was uneasy with the relation between dialogue and evangelism expressed in the resolutions and the document: 'Those who are most interested in dialogue tend to be soft on evangelism; those who are most interested in evangelism perhaps tend to be soft on the need for dialogue. In our consideration of these two motions in this section, we are having the emphasis almost wholly the one way. It is significant that evangelism came in as an afterthought, accepted as an addition to the motion as a result of a proposed amendment.' He wished that the Conference had been able to combine these concerns, and that in the editorial process an attempt would be made to establish very significant links between these two important areas of witness.

Asking Jews for forgiveness

At the press conference the question was also raised whether the Conference would make a statement asking for forgiveness from Jews for the holocaust. This was resisted on a number of grounds. First, one of the authors of *Jews, Christians and Muslims*, Bishop Richard Harries, insisted that: 'forgiveness implies an acceptance of personal responsibility for which you personally are asking. Most people in the world were not alive at the time of the holocaust. What we are talking about is the acceptance by the Christian tradition of the dark side of its history as well as its light side. There are very strong statements [in the document] calling Christianity to a profound, painful re-examination of its relationship with Judaism. I do not think the word forgiveness is necessarily appropriate.'

There was a very definite resistance from the Two Thirds World. The Bishop of Jerusalem, Bishop Samir Kaffity, had a clear reason for opposing such a move: 'Not all Christians were involved in the holocaust. This was a local problem for Europe and not for elsewhere. We all condemn the holocaust and what the Jewish people underwent over here on this continent at the time when they had found refuge and better relationships with their cousins elsewhere. But we cannot generalize and ask all the Christians of the world to seek forgiveness for a thing they did not cause. If you want to think that the Christians are represented by the Christians of Europe, that is another story. But there are more Christians than in Europe.'

Archbishop Khotso Makhulu of Central Africa was clear that the problem should first be set in a wider context. 'For the region from which I have come, talks of the holocaust and corporate repentance would be unhelpful. We speak as a communion and keep on saying that the Anglican Communion is growing in many parts of the world which have not had a share in the history of the last world war. It is very difficult for us to be dragged in to that kind of situation. If we go for a pound for pound situation we would have to go into the history of slavery and ask for repentance in all quarters.'

There was some unhappiness with a resolution to commend the document as it stood. This was voiced in an amendment which was carried, proposed by the Archbishop of Melbourne, Bishop David Penman, an Islamic scholar, and Bishop Samir Kaffity. Bishop Kaffity put the following points: 'I come from the land which gave birth to Judaism, Christianity and Islam, the three of them having Semitic roots before Europe was baptized into the Christian faith. The Christian faith was born into my country. These three faiths existed side by side in history with a great deal of mutual respect and understanding, until beyond their control they have been exploited by secular forces. We would like these three faiths to contribute to the world humanity as they did before.

'Though it is difficult to have very objective talks, yet we encourage dialogue to be divorced from partisan politics or incidents in the life of the peoples, be they Jews, Arabs, Muslims or Christians—dialogue for dialogue's sake. With a lot in common between these three Semitic faiths, this document could not in the short time allotted for its preparation explore all the major points of understanding, affirmation or sharing, specially where these faiths co-exist. It produced some good points but it is incomplete. Therefore I support the slight amendment given by Archbishop David Penman, which will commend this paper for further study, by not only academicians and scholars on Islam and Judaism within our communion, whom we need, but by ordinary Anglicans co-existing in an inter-religious society where the three Abrahamic faiths exist side by side. The working party should be representative of the whole communion and not just one segment of it. Hopefully one such working party with Islam and Judaism only will produce their common agenda. We cannot force an agenda on our counterpart in the dialogue. The agenda should be a product of our coming together.'

Shariah law

There had been a number of pleas in the plenary session on African issues for help for those Christian minorities living in Africa under Shariah law. Bishop Samir Kaffity spoke on this point in the press conference: 'We have a lot of ignorance about Shariah law. Perhaps it was once applied in certain places. But as it stands there is a lot of consultation in Shariah law. There are a lot of rules for non-Muslims to enjoy their rights. There are places where Shariah law is applied and where Christians are enjoying the maximum of their liberty.'

Archbishop David Penman made the point that, 'where Shariah law is applied unjustly and inhumanely, it is as bad as where Christian principles are applied inadequately. It is a little easy for this conference to condemn Shariah law out of hand.'

Bishop Harries also spoke on this point in the press conference: 'A very important paragraph in the Jewish Muslim document is indicative of the whole approach pointing out that within Shariah law there is proper allowance for religious minorities to practise their religion. It is not a question of imposing a Western concept of human rights upon Muslims, it is a question of reminding Muslims of what is actually there within Shariah.'[1]

The document states: 'Islamic law, Shariah, is based on the belief that God has, as a gracious act of mercy, revealed to humanity basic guidelines to live both individually and in society. Whereas Christians tend today to think of Christian faith as a personal commitment which can be expressed quite happily in a secular society, many Muslims believe that God has revealed his will on how the whole of society is to be ordered, from details of banking to matters of public health. ... Some non-Muslim communities living under Shariah Islamic rule experience the application of Shariah law as oppressive and inhumane. Another aspect of Shariah law that causes some distress is the treatment of women. We note that in many respects Islamic law has pioneered the rights of women. For example under Islamic law married women had the right to own property and conduct business in their own names thirteen centuries before these rights were granted in many Western countries. It is hoped that Christians and Muslims may search together for ways in which the position of women may continue to be improved for the benefit of society as a whole. We also need to remember that classical Islamic law provides safeguards for the rights of religious minorities which are not actually being enforced today. Further, in judging we must always be careful to compare like with like. We must compare the highest and most humane ideals of Islam with the highest and most humane ideals of Christianity and the misuse of power at the hands of Muslims with the misuse of power at the hands of those who call themselves Christians.'

Assessment

During the debate on the report on dialogue with Muslims and Jews, Bishop David Young of Ripon signalled an important protest that there was no reflection or discussion with Buddhism. He identified a major omission in the Lambeth agenda. For the dialogue with Islam and Judaism is essentially a dialogue with two other monotheistic religions. It is also an internal dialogue within the Semitic family of religions, since Islam and Christianity share common roots in Judaism. Except for Islam, which claims 800 million adherents, dialogue with the religions of the remaining 3.2 billion people in the world is a dialogue with religious pluralism. Religious pluralism was not addressed at Lambeth, but was a context for many of the bishops.

Religious pluralism

Religious pluralism is an important challenge to the Christian faith. The conference at Tambaram in January 1988 to celebrate the fiftieth anniversary of the world missionary conference at Tambaram in 1938, identified that pluralism was top of the agenda for discussion by the Churches. The conference identified the following important agenda items for the future: 'In what ways is plurality, including religious plurality, within God's purpose? Is the nature of reality itself plural? In a plural world can we know God and truth and be self-confident without ignoring or disdaining our fellows? Can we recognize God-given faith different from our own? What role do we give to the voices of our neighbours of other faiths and to their contributions to faith as we face the future together? How does our life with people of other faiths affect the faiths affect the content of our theology and its methodology? In what ways does it raise questions about the starting points, assumption and authority for doing theology and for education within the Church? How does the plurality of theologies within the Christian community itself affect our response to the wider religious plurality? How do the confessions in other religions of decisiveness/universality/uniqueness challenge and clarify Christian convictions about the uniqueness of Christ? Christians affirm that salvation is offered to the whole creation through Jesus Christ. In a pluralistic world where there are different understandings of liberation and the human predicament, how can we be clearer about what salvation means? What do we say about the saving work of God through other religious traditions? In what ways does our understanding of God as Trinity enable us to explore the work of God? For this, do we need a fuller understanding of the role of the Holy Spirit? In what ways can or must the work of God be discerned outside the boundaries of the Church? What is the mission of God outside those boundaries? What is the role of social and religious movements in the work or mission of God? What implications do they have for our understanding of mission and dialogue? And where does the preferential option for the poor figure in the context of dialogue?'[2]

These questions raise the challenge of Christian uniqueness. In *The Myth of Christian Uniqueness*,[3] edited by John Hick and Paul Knitter, contributors argue that claims of Christian uniqueness came out of the context when Western culture was dominant, and thus considered itself superior on all fronts—science, technology, philosophy, morals and religion. They suggest that there is now a near reversal of that situation. Other religions have achieved at least parity. 'Western religion became one among the other world religions; and (not insignificantly) the Christian faith became the one now most morally culpable, the chief imperialistic, non-spiritual and in fact barely moral faith. . . . Christianity now stood not as the accuser but as the morally accused by other religions.'[4]

This analysis does not give adequate attention to the claims of Christian uniqueness in the Christian tradition before Constantine, nor to the experience of non-Western ancient Churches in Asia and Africa where, in most cases, Christianity was not part of a dominant culture but was often powerless and weak in worldly terms. None of these Churches ever compromised their belief in Christian uniqueness in these circumstances.

Mission in the context of other faiths

A number of approaches have been discerned to the relationship between Christianity and other religions. There is the exclusive approach which, in its best sense, gives Christ an exclusive place as the one anointed by God to bring the kingdom of God into history, and to deal with human sin and cosmic evil through his atoning death on the cross and his resurrection. Any relationship that people may have with God must consciously or unconsciously be related to Christ. There is also the approach that accepts the exclusive claims of Christ, but suggests that people of other religions are saved in their own religious contexts through Christ's unacknowledged presence in them. The context of pluralism is seeking to move the Church to an inclusive approach which, at its strongest, gives all religions an equal validity in their claims to mediate the truth of God.

Some bishops saw other religions in the context of good and evil, light and dark, with no shades of grey. Such a perspective tends to evaluate cultures and religions as either good or bad. It either accommodates totally to a culture—for example, to some versions of North American free enterprise—or reacts totally against it. Thus, a very valuable holy table embellished with a symbol of a dragon was recently destroyed in Singapore Cathedral. Such a perspective tends to see other religions as fundamentally expressions of the occult; it analyses the occult in terms of power, and then calls on Christians to demonstrate the greater power of the strong man (Christ) who binds. From this perspective, healing crusades and ministries of deliverance are prime expressions of evangelism in the context of both secular and religious societies.

Other bishops came with a different understanding. Bishop Michael Nazir-Ali, the director of studies for the Conference, had eighteen months previously chaired the drafting committee of a World Council of Churches' Conference on Evangelism at which Bishop David Gitari played a major role. Their report read as follows:

'Authentic witness to Jesus Christ should be carried out in a spirit of respect for the beliefs and devotion of others. It can never be simply a "telling", but must also be a sensitive "listening". . . . We acknowledge that God has not left himself without witness anywhere (Acts 17.16) and we joyfully recognize a knowledge of God, a sense of the transcendent, among many human communities, including faith communities. At the same time, it needs to be pointed out that humankind's knowledge of God is vitiated by sin and God's gracious revelation in Christ is needed to call us back to an authentic vision of God.

'The proclamation of the gospel includes an invitation to each person to recognize and accept in a personal decision the saving Lordship of Christ. This might be seen as a fulfilment of the aspirations of humankind expressed sometimes in religious traditions but at other times in non-religious movements and even at times in counter-religious movements. Such proclamation may also be understood as a making explicit of an implicit knowledge; or as bringing assurance and certainty of salvation to all those who, without prior explicit knowledge of Jesus Christ, the only Saviour and Lord, have nevertheless realized their own inadequacy and sin and have thrown themselves on the mercy of God.'[5]

In the Asian context, the home of pluralistic religions, the issue of dialogue with non-Christian religions cannot omit the question of how they relate to the poor. Examination of the ministry of Jesus as recorded in the Gospels suggests that when he was discussing with religious leaders, the issue for discussion was not their own personal spiritual experience but the way the practice of their religion marginalized 'sinners', the poor and the sick. The pluralism of Indian religions means that the questions of the poor about their lot are all relativized; there is no final basis on which they can call their situation unjust or wrong. The impact of Christianity is to give the poor a foundation for their questions in the will and purpose of God; to affirm the poor in their sense of injustice and their desire and hope for change; to give them a new identity—not initially in a changed society, but in a new relationship with God in Christ as his children and called equally to steward his creation.

Notes

1. See further Michael Nazir-Ali, *Martyrs and Magistrates: Toleration and Trial in Islam* (Bramcote, Nottingham, Grove Booklets on Ethics, 1989).

2. From Jean Stromberg, 'Christian Witness in a Pluralistic World' (*International Review of Mission*, July 1988) pp.412 ff.

3. John Hick and Paul Knitter (eds), *The Myth of Christian Uniqueness* (London, SCM Press, 1987).

4. Langdon Gilkey, 'Plurality and its Theological Implications', in ibid., p. 40.

5. See 'The Stuttgart Statement', in *Proclaiming Christ in Christ's Way*, ed. by Vinay Samuel and Albrecht Hauser (Oxford, Regnum Books, 1989).

CHAPTER 6

Women and the Media

The issue of the consecration of women to the episcopate high-lighted the way that the media creates, highlights and shapes an issue to take centre stage at an event such as the Lambeth Conference.

During the summer of 1988, BBC Radio in the United Kingdom conducted two investigations into the attempts of women to gain admittance to the male bastions of Richmond Golf Club and the pavilion of the Lancashire County Cricket Club. There was at least one honest man interviewed, who admitted the rules existed in order to give him and his fellows a break from their womenfolk.

His bluntness identified an important psychological dimension to the issue of the ordination of women: some men seem to need space on their own. The army, single-sex education, and sport are all areas of British life where men have created their own clubs. Women have complained that where such a club has a role in mediating between women and their God from whom they derive their humanity and identity, it militates against the humanization which the gospel brings.

The bishops of the Anglican Communion are *de facto* one of the most exclusive men's clubs in the world. To use theological argument to penetrate such a bastion, is not all that easy. The experience of the ages, that men like space on their own, was never admitted or explored as a factor in the whole debate.

Consecration of women to the episcopate

From the British media's point of view, the most significant debate in the Conference focused on whether women would be admitted to the order of bishops. The issue was seen by many as an issue of culture, emerging from societies where the sexual revolution and the liberation of women set the agenda. The North Americans would claim that this was an issue not of culture but of gospel, a first-order issue where, once you had the right theology, the action would follow. Others argued that it was not just an issue of theology. They would reflect on the theology but it was also an issue of culture.

The Reverend Nan Peete

Certainly the proponents of women's ordination had a winner in the Reverend Nan Peete. She came from the right background to disarm some theological opposition—as a black woman priest in an Anglo-Catholic parish. She gave a moving account of her own ministry, drawing deeply on her experience.

She disavowed any intention to engage in a theological exercise over the validity of her orders or to present an apologetic for who or what she was. It was her intention to share the breadth and scope, the joys and pains of being a priest in a wonderful and wonder-filled Church.

'In the fullness of time God called me from one ministry to another; from many active years of ministry as a lay person in the Church and in the community, to the ordained ministry in the Church and in the community. In obedience to God's call and in faithfulness to God, I answered that call. Understanding my call to be to this community, I knew that it must be validated by that community. Ministry is not done in isolation. It is to and from a faith community. I again was blessed with laity, clergy and bishops who supported and validated that call.

'The sacramental nature of my priesthood is acknowledged by many of the black male ministers who call me their priest and confessor as one they trust. Episcopal priests as well as Roman Catholic priests and sisters seek me out for spiritual direction.'

Through her moving speech people heard her cry and felt her pain. She became a media focus and her face appeared in many newspapers. But even the media sometimes misses important aspects of the news. We saw no mention of the fact that, though she looked not a day over twenty-nine, she was in fact fifty-one and a grandmother.

The vision of God

From a theological point of view, some of the most incisive

theological presentations in the Conference came from two women, Mrs Elizabeth Templeton and Dr Elizabeth Coakley. Elizabeth Templeton spoke brilliantly of an outsider's view of the Anglican Communion. Dr Coakley identified that a major issue underlying the debate about women's ordination was the issue of the vision of God. Did she overstate her case, however, and suggest that the whole tale of Christian theology for the last 2,000 years has been distorted by a patriarchal model of God?

It was remarkable how, given the small number of women engaged in the ordained ministry of the Church and seeking the episcopate, this issue brings such a dominant challenge from the intricate details of canon law right up to the very understanding of God.

In their presentation, the women pointed out that the challenge of Christian women was not basically about the ordination of women to the priesthood or the episcopate, or storming the places of power and decision-making. The challenges belong together: they form an 'interlocking agenda'. At the heart of the matter was a challenge to the vision of God. The central question to the Church is: 'Whatever you mean to do, are you in fact presenting to the world a vision of God which is too small?' They wanted to know how it was possible for all Christians to talk about God in such a way that women were made to feel that they too were equal members of God's family.

Elizabeth Coakley made the case in the following way: 'Behind and beneath every political, economic and social question with which women theologians and their opponents struggle today, is a deeper and more profound question about our vision of God. For this it is that informs and inspires our quest for a more equitable, more just and above all more holy and true understanding of the relationship between men and women in the Church. . . . I suggest that the way we actually visualize the inner workings of the persons of the Trinity, the way we project their power relations, their sexual identity, their mode of operating together: all this is powerfully illuminating of what we then take to be normative for the community of women and men in the Church, and their relationships. We are talking then of that rich level of imaginative symbolism which, however unconsciously, does inform our faith.

'It is no coincidence that it is in the mystics, those given most determinedly and constantly to prayer, that insistent questions about the integration of sexuality often daringly find their voice. And with that sometimes goes a felt need for a compensatory projection on to the Godhead of what our society calls 'feminine' attributes, alongside the hallowed 'masculine' ones; only with this, it is felt, can we approach an adequate vision of *God* and so, with that, an accompanying vision of wholeness for humanity.'

The major question for the proponents of women's ordination was how one man alone can be the symbol of unity. For the opponents, the idea of a woman bishop was a contradiction in terms.

The bishops' reactions

Many bishops had hesitancies about the way in which the issue was presented and the debate conducted. A Two Thirds World bishop wrote: 'The women's presentation was pretty counter-productive and far too concerned with the wrong issues. There is room for taking a much more affirmative view of the role women have traditionally fulfilled in the West as in parts of the Third World. Far too high a profile was given to the issue of women's ordination to the episcopate. For those for whom the issue is relevant the arguments were largely well known.' Bishop John Taylor of St Albans thought that the Conference took one step forward in having a good number of women as advisers and consultants. But one step back because the women's presentation was counter-productive and, at times, disagreeably feminist and sadly humourless.

Bishop Fitzsimons Allison from North America thought that it was salutary to see first hand, bishops from truly tragic areas relating the enormous crises the Church is facing, which then puts 'women's ordination' in some perspective. Even if no minds were changed, the priorities were changed.

Proponents of women's ordination were also hesitant. Roger Herfft from New Zealand was disappointed that there was no celebration of women's ministry, and many women commented that they felt spoken about by men as objects. Maurice Goodall regretted the general lack of real biblical debate on the subject. David Evans of Peru, an opponent of women's ordination, felt that 'no genuine theological issues were faced, and that everything was discussed on the basis of experience'.

Another bishop commented: 'Entrenched positions are still held on both sides. However, the resolution passed was very helpful. If ministry of women is to be given its correct place, more space is to be made in the Conference itself. Women should be part of the plenary sessions.'

The Conference decision was to leave the real decision to a commission. For if women were to be ordained to the episcopate, as some provinces insisted they would be in the near future, how would those ordained or confirmed by women bishops be received in provinces where such ordinations were not recognized? Would the Anglican Communion in fact become three communions—one of those ordaining women to the episcopate in communion with each other, a second one not ordaining women in communion with each other, and a non-aligned group of those in communion with both, headed by the Archbishop of Canterbury. When this scenario was suggested to the Archbishop in a press conference, he did not reply that the analysis was incorrect, just premature, as the commission had not yet reported. But that was exactly the question that the Conference was faced with, and neatly ducked by passing it to the commission.

The Wives' Conference

The Bishops' Wives' Conference was held a mile away at St Edward's School, to which the bishops' wives made their way each day from their accommodation with their husbands at the University of Kent.

In each of their three weeks together (in contrast to one week in 1978), they looked at the family, women in the Church and women in the world. The context of women in the Two Thirds World was starkly set out on the last but one day of their conference.

Rajamani Rowley told how, in the Two Thirds World, crushing poverty overlaid with long-standing discrimination make living conditions for millions of women almost too harsh to imagine. They perform two-thirds of the world's work, receive one-tenth of its income, and own less than one-hundredth of its property. From birth to death a woman's status is a derived one—her destiny is defined in relation to being a daughter, a wife and a mother. Many women in the Third World carry triple workloads—in their households, labour in the fields, and their reproductive roles. Yet, according to statistics, they are not working. Women carry 90 per cent of the water in Africa, gather most of the fuel, grow half the world's food but get no credit facilities and no training. In the Two Thirds World, 25 million women suffer serious complications in childbirth; in some societies by the age of five girl mortality is double that of boys because, in the allocation of food, men and boys eat first. Some 75 per cent of illiterates are women. But the hope lies in women. As one woman put it: 'Without us women, Africa will never develop. The development of Africa rests on my hands. By ignoring me as a woman you are damaging my self-esteem. But I struggle on because I know Africa will never develop without me.' Women hold the key to family health, child survival, proper resource management, the slowing down of population growth, without which there is no hope in India, Africa and many other parts of our interdependent world.

A gifted African social worker pointed out to us earlier that the only omission from such a presentation was the factor that in many societies poverty strengthens the role of women. Men have to leave the farms to seek work in the cities, and thus become marginal to the well-being of their families. The marginalization of men must be set alongside the feminization of poverty.

What in particular did the bishops' wives bring with them? Susan Chang Him from the Seychelles brought a feeling of isolation, and how she dealt with the feeling of living a thousand miles away from the next bishop's wife.

The Nigerian wives brought their experience of the extended family. In the discussions on hospices and care of the old, they said that they did not have such things in Nigeria. It is very important in Nigeria that your mother dies in your lap, and your father dies at home.

Bible Studies—another hit

All the wives we spoke to identified the Bible Studies as the highlight of their conference. For Janet Wesonga from Uganda, it was the most exciting part of the conference, as every member of the group was given an opportunity to express what she felt about the subject under study. Susan Chang Him found the studies a fantastic opportunity to share experiences and cultures alongside the text of the Bible. They studied the women in the Bible—

Martha, Mary, Salome—and each one said in her own way how this fitted in with their country and life. Judith Luxmoor from Bermuda found the African wives much more spiritual than the Western ones. They were much more geared to reading the Bible and Bible Study, and discussing religion, than Western wives were.

Worship

All greatly appreciated the service at the end of the wives' conference. One wife described it for us: 'I felt very moved by the worship. We prayed for hope and peace in the world. The Lord's prayer was expressed by liturgical dance by wives of the bishops who had learnt it during the conference and performed it for the first time. At the end of the worship Mrs Runcie released a white dove as a symbol of peace, followed by the release of another 150 doves. It was beautiful and very moving.'

Susan Chang Him spoke warmly of the liturgical dance of the Lord's prayer, and its value in making her think much more than when just repeating it verbally. Seeing it made it mean so much more. She plans to introduce it at the next confirmation service in order to show how movement can explain God's word.

When the bishops were having their fast, it was not possible for the lunch arrangements to be cancelled at the wives' conference. So they made creative use of the opportunity and ate lunch in silence with a fast on talking. 'It was so different from our usual talking and laughing and cheering; it was a silence in solidarity with those people who do not have.'

But Jean Penman from Melbourne was disappointed there was no time for more informal expression of worship. There seemed very little opportunity for those with a charismatic orientation to express themselves freely in worship. Everything was set in such English structures.

Loneliness

The wives spent time reflecting on the role of a bishop's wife. Many found their position lonely. In some cases there is a general feeling that people miss being in parish situations, from which most of the wives have come. Jean Penman told us: 'Once you become a bishop's wife you are cut off from this sort of family set-up in the parish, and that has come out very clearly. Whereas the bishops have their clergy to relate to, there is nothing for the bishops' wives to relate to. They did not feel that they had a vicar anymore.'

The African bishops' wives have a different role. They have much more of a teaching role, instructing the clergy wives in family planning, and in how to keep their houses clean. They are often treated like queens. Some explained that it was so hard for them to go to a gathering where everyone is sitting on the floor, and yet there is one chair for them. They have great problems not wanting to be singled out culturally.

There were three presentations by bishops' wives who had their own separate jobs. It was felt that it would also be helpful to have had a presentation by someone who did not have a separate outside job, but spent her time helping her husband.

All those wives we spoke with regretted that there was no interaction with the male conference, particularly in the discussions of women's ordination and polygamy. Apart from being issues that affected women, the wives felt that they had particular insights to share with the bishops.

Susan Chang Him felt that if a person is called to be ordained, the time will come when they will be ordained. Women come as the persons they are and, if they are sincerely called, they will become priests. She did not like it when they were fighting for the issue.

Judith Luxmoor felt the lobbyists for women's ordination had taken it for granted that all the women were supportive of women's ordination since all the lobbying efforts had been concentrated on the bishops where opinion was divided. She was sure that a woman could do the job much better than a man because women have more sensitivity. But for her, it was a question of until the whole Church agrees to do it, the step should not be taken.

One bishop's wife from Latin America explained how she related to God as Father as part of her Christian relating to God. She was very hurt by the suggestion in the women's presentation at the male conference that she had been conned and had a distorted patriarchal view. To Judith Luxmoor, God is male, Christ was male, and the feminine side she did not understand.

The Nigerian women were concerned about the pastoral problems women's ordination would present to them. How would a single woman priest, living in the pastor's compound, relate to the pastor's wife? If she is married and is transferred to another church, what happens to the children and their education?

Janet Wesonga wondered if for a woman with five or six children, it was really fair for her to be ordained. She particularly felt that a lot of African women would have liked to have discussed the issue of polygamy. Her own view was that in the issue of polygamy, a man had to choose. Jesus said go and sell everything if you want to follow me; but now the Church seemed to be saying, 'do not sell your things, you can stay as you want'. For some women who have been forced into polygamy, to be sent away is a liberation.

So it began to seem to one bishop's wife that the consultants did the theology, the bishops voted on it, and the wives had nothing to do with it at all. Jean Penman felt that it would be excellent to have expertise flowing both ways between the conferences.

There was warm appreciation for the practical workshops. Susan Chang Him thought that some bishops would do well to attend some of the workshops—for instance, the ones on communication and the use of the media. The workshops on family planning were very useful for her work in marriage preparation. Workshops were not about influencing government policy, but about how Christian families are built up as a sort of counter-force to the invasion of Westernization. One lady said, 'I would like you all to come to my diocese, so please come as quickly as possible since Westernization and tourism will wreck it in the next twenty-five years.'

A resources exhibition enabled bishops' wives to see what was available, and the work of various organizations was much appreciated.

Snatches of fun and humour percolated up to the men's conference. Like the time when Rosalind Runcie was finding it hard to encourage her guests at the palace in Canterbury to go home at the end of an evening, and so started a conga from the party which eventually wound out to the buses! And the time when Leah Tutu asked each participant to turn to her neighbour, shake her hand and say, 'My husband is a good boy'—and then, 'And I am a better girl'.

Taking Lambeth with them

Janet Wesonga will take back the encouragement to clergy wives to keep together as clergy wives, pray for one another and see what they can do together. She felt that clergy wives expect people to do something for them, but do not help themselves.

Susan Chang Him will take back the feeling of belonging to such a big family; memories of the beauty of being at Lambeth, living and sharing with sisters in Christ from all four corners of the earth: 'We are all one big family. We may have problems, or different opinions, that also happens in families. But we are united in love and prayer and the truth of our Lord Jesus Christ. We can sustain each other in prayer. I shall still be isolated one thousand miles from the nearest bishop's wife, but I go back feeling that I am not alone, there are many of us and a lot of us with the same feeling of isolation which will be no more because I know that with all these prayers we will be nearer each other; and meeting all these people I have heard about, like Desmond Tutu, brings to life all the people we pray for in the Anglican cycle of prayer. I feel closer now to the reality of the different problems and when I pray or we pray I shall be able to put faces and lives to the names.'

The media culture

Bishops arriving at Lambeth were surprised at the dismissive attitude of the British media to the Lambeth Conference, its hostility to the Church of England in general and to Robert Runcie in particular. Of course, the majority of the press in England appears to be right wing and to reject the critical stance that the Church of England leadership has taken towards the British government, especially over the Falklands war and the inner cities. The Bishop of Durham is on record as calling some of the government's policies 'evil'.

A group of thirty-two bishops from Australia wrote the following letter to the *Lambeth Daily* newspaper: 'We frankly have a suspicion that this failure of the secular press to "get it right" may result from the tendency of some journalists to write to a preconceived formula, from which they are unwilling to free themselves, but perhaps under an unconscious but understandable pressure of need to fulfil their own gloomy pre-Lambeth prophecies. Alternatively, perhaps they are tending to interpret the functioning of the Anglican Communion from the perspective of a far too narrowly English set of past experiences. If any journalist would like to make contact with us we shall as a group be pleased to do our bit to help connect them with what has actually been going on.'

One example of their complaints is that on a day of significant discussions at the Conference, the *Daily Telegraph* led with an article about a leaflet by a small right-wing group that had been distributed to all the bishops and accused the Church of England of left-wing bias. When the *Daily Telegraph* man on the spot was challenged about this, he replied that while he had included the leaflet in his report, it was his editorial department that had given it prominence.

The journalists, or rather one journalist, Walter Schwarz of the *Guardian*, responded to the bishops' request and met the bishops for a press conference in reverse, with the Australian bishops asking the questions. It was most unfortunate that Clifford Longley of *The Times*, who had suggested the time of the meeting, failed to appear, Andrew Brown of the *Independent* came in fifteen minutes late, and the *Telegraph* man never showed up at all. We know this to be true because one of us was there. Walter Schwarz ably defended his corner. He had a legitimate complaint that the press arrangements at the Conference so protected the bishops that a whole series of in-depth interviews he had planned with Two Thirds World bishops had to be cancelled because he could never find any of the bishops or fix appointments with them. He also had a legitimate point that the English secular press were not religious newspapers, and had to survive by selling newspapers to secular people in Britain. Thus issues that interested British people—like would their next vicar or bishop be a woman—would be dominant. However, the Australians were hardly pacified in their view that the press seemed to have taken a particularly negative view of the Conference, the communion and the Archbishop which was hardly justified by the facts.

The one who did most to undermine the credibility of the British press was Robert Runcie. His role at the Conference, and the affection he inspired (which found its climax when all the primates joined him on the stage at the end of his closing address and embraced him warmly), raised the question as to whether this man had been fairly presented to the world through the eyes of the British press. Bishop Timothy Dudley-Smith of Thetford, England, commented: 'I felt the Conference has been a personal triumph, under God, for the Archbishop of Canterbury. I do not see how the British press can go on picturing him as an ineffective and isolated leader presiding over the dissolution of the Anglican Communion.'

The press could have discovered that in the very process of the Conference, their own standards of critical judgement of religion and politics were focused on the Anglican Church and world political leaders by Anglican bishops themselves. In this way, they could have discovered the contribution of the Church of England to the world in its unwillingness to legitimize political power, in contrast to the tendency in all religious traditions to legitimize it. Anglican Churches throughout the world had never taken orders from England, had always been national churches, making their own decisions and so were always able from a tradition of being independent to call political power to account. The British press could have seen that the best traditions of a free press were actually being carried out by this international gathering in their own contexts and Conference.

This autonomy was as a result of the spiritual strength of the Anglican bishops because they were never dependent on the state. The Anglican Communion is truly in spirit and resources independent of state power. Its willingness to uphold the important instrument of bringing political power to accountability lies here and not in political systems, Parliament, democracy, or even a secular press. The fact that the British press could not see this, suggests that the press reporters themselves were finding it difficult to be their own men and women, and that secularism is not a sufficient assurance of autonomy.

The international impact of the Conference was demonstrated in the way in which Bishop David Gitari's call for a change in the stance on polygamy was reported. First, it was misreported. The Reuters' correspondent, who was a young girl in her twenties sitting next to us in the press gallery, sent off a report in which she claimed that Bishop Gitari was advocating polygamy. The Kenyan *Daily Nation* picked up this report and ran a story the following day, on 27 July, under the heading 'Gitari recommends polygamy in church'—'A Kenyan bishop has told Anglican leaders that

Christians should be allowed to have more than one wife and urged the Church to baptize polygamists.'

That morning on the streets of Embu, the centre of Bishop Gitari's diocese, everyone was talking about his comments. One man ran about declaring that he was going to have many wives because the bishop said he could. The bishop's colleagues acted fast. They pulled a copy of his text out of the diocesan computer, drove to Nairobi and went round every newspaper office with the correct version of his speech. On 29 July, the *Daily Nation* ran a piece headed: 'What I actually said—Gitari', which pointed out, 'the story filed by Reuters and published in Kenya was inaccurate. They denied that the prelate ever spoke to Reuters.'

The President of Kenya commented on television that he was surprised at Bishop Gitari's call which he thought to be against Christian doctrine. The inaccuracy of the Reuters' report handed more ammunition to those in Kenya who wanted to undermine the position of Bishop Gitari in his concern for justice in political life. But Bishop Gitari's colleagues also pointed out that the need to correct the report meant that the full thrust of what he had actually said was reported two days later throughout the Kenyan press.

Head for the rocks please

The best description of the role of the press came in New Zealander Peter Davis's closing briefing to the bishops as they returned to face their own press. The Conference had been like a ship which, about three weeks ago, 'was being tossed on a heavy sea. Gunboats gathered, helicopters hovered, periscopes popped up. The British press had arrived. I lived with this image for the first few days. It developed like a cartoon of the mind. In a helicopter above the vessel, a photographer called out, "Could you head for the rocks? We'd prefer an action photograph." I was told the introduction of the British press to this Conference was all pretty normal fare and something to do with the "anything goes pluralism" of Britain where Jesus is Lord, Allah is great and Rupert Murdoch [son of a devout Australian Anglican] is doing fine.' Peter Davis had sized them up by the end.

For Canon Samuel van Culin, Conference secretary, this inter-action was part of the concrete witness of the gospel in context. For a number of Two Thirds World bishops, the Conference was an important exposure to the power of the media in modern society. It encouraged them to work on developing a creative relationship with media in their own context.

It was also quite clear that the Two Thirds World bishops were intrigued by the way the Lambeth Conference itself wooed the media. The role of the media was seen as fundamental to propagating the concerns of the Conference. As the secular media is so much more powerful in presence and technology than the religious media, this meant that the secular media gained dominance. Its concerns dictated the timing and, increasingly, the very agenda of the Conference. It was obvious that, to the Two Thirds World bishops, this was a fact of modern Western society. The questions were raised as to how much such dominance by the media restricted space for the non-Western concerns to get highlighted, and impact the life of the communion. We have already noted in our discussion of reception, the very real possibility that the media could have a highly significant role in any process of reception of a doctrine in the Church. This could further stifle the contribution of non-Western or minority concerns.

It seemed as if there was a contextualization taking place in the Conference. For an international conference, the most important aspect of the Conference appeared to be the secular Western press. Should this not figure prominently in the agenda for the preparatory committee for the next Lambeth Conference?

CHAPTER 7

Talking about God

'Theology is always a language about God'. With these words Gustavo Gutierrez, the father of liberation theology, focused his presentation to the Lambeth Conference. 'A great part of modern theology is how to answer this question: how to speak about God in a world in which God seems unnecessary.' He struck a familiar and welcome chord with many bishops.

For they had primarily gathered not as a synod or council to legislate and make decisions. Anglican bishops are called to be upholders and teachers of the faith. Bishop Michael Nazir-Ali from Pakistan, the director of studies for the Conference, had said in the pre-Conference preparation process that, 'because it has been thought that the primary task of a bishop is to teach, the Lambeth Conference is concerned much more to evaluate Christian teaching on a whole number of areas and then to set out guidelines on those issues on which Christians need guidance'. However, we are told that in some provinces the chief credential for being a bishop is the ability to administer in the midst of the conflicting struggles of various interest groups. But the major justification for holding the Conference was as a theological forum for teachers of the Church. This dimension greatly impressed Bishop Victor Premasagar, the moderator of the Church of South India, himself a theologian, who was attending Lambeth for the first time. He was greatly encouraged by the fact that bishops could take so much time to discuss theological issues. The fact that the chief pastors of the Church could meet to share theological insights and concerns and be equipped theologically is a very special contribution that the United Churches in South Asia need, and that other non-Catholic denominations do not as yet have.

The problem facing the bishops was how, in the various contexts in which they and their people found themselves, could they talk about God. How did they do this at Lambeth?

How to talk about God:

Among women

The women were, in a sense, crying out for a God-talk that makes them feel that God's justice and love embraces them; that s/he is ours; that the he and she aspect are both highlighted; that is not beyond but embraces both sexes.

Where God is irrelevant

David Jenkins's presentation on evangelism had identified that the fundamental issue for him was how to talk about God in a society where traditional language about God is not widely accepted or seen as relevant. In this context, he proposed to begin with God: 'The central issue which provides the base for evangelism is "who do we believe God to be and what do we believe God to be doing?" The central issue and content of the gospel is not Jesus but God.' For Bishop Jenkins, the starting point was not Jesus as one who reveals God, but God.

Amidst religious pluralism

Professor Stanley Samartha spoke from the context of inter-religious dialogue. In responding to Archbishop Keith Rayner's address on authority, he focused on the diverse images that Christians hold of Jesus and on the different conclusions they reach when the same Holy Spirit brings to remembrance the things of Jesus. From the diversity within Christian tradition, he argued that one Christian tradition cannot be imposed on other Christian traditions, and extrapolated that the authority of one religious tradition cannot be imposed on neighbours of other faiths who live by their own authorities.

He set the issue of God-talk in the context of the plurality of religions. His fundamental question was whether the criteria developed within a community of faith on the basis of one particular scripture, can be used to pass judgements on the faiths of those who have other scriptures as their authority.

Among the poor

Gustavo Gutierrez, a parish priest of a slum congregation in Peru and a university lecturer, gave a major plenary presentation to the Conference. He identified a reality common to many Two Thirds World situations when he asked how it was possible to affirm to the suffering and innocent poor that God loved them.

He said: 'For the poor people in the world, and normally I am speaking from, above all, my own context but am conscious of the fact that many of these affirmations are good for all the areas of the world. For us the question is rather how to speak about God from the suffering of the innocent. Innocent in this case is not synonymous with non-sinner. All persons are sinners. Innocent means those who do not merit or deserve their present suffering. In other words, our question, it seems to me, is how to say to poor persons "God loves you". It is for us, for many people today in the world, the big question. This question seems to have an aspect linked to preaching. I think Karl Barth has taught us that there is not a big difference between preaching and doing theology. Because theology is a language on God. For us it is the big question, how to say to the poor and insignificant, to the last in the world, "God loves you", when all in daily life seems to deny the presence of the love of God.'

In Africa

The question of how to talk about God did not surface in most of the African presentations in the same way that it did with the others. It did not sound as though the Africans had grappled with these questions. But three situations pose the question starkly. First, the struggles of the South African situation raise the question as to how it is possible to talk about God when, in the name of God, so many atrocities are committed of violence, of separation of men from their families, and of tribal rivalries.

Secondly, in the face of aggressive Islam, there is the struggle to recover God who brings transformation in contrast to a God who imposes his own culture. Lamin Sanneh[1] identifies the crucial issue of vernacularization. In Islamic contexts, God-talk is often bound up with an imposed culture. Bishop Michael Nazir-Ali describes how on a visit to Nigeria before Lambeth, he went to a mosque where there were streams of people worshipping. But they had to call on him to translate the Arabic verses carved on the walls of the mosque as the Nigerian Muslims were surrounded by religious art and symbolism they could not understand.

The case of Uganda poses the question of God-talk starkly. Some eighty per cent of the population are Christian. But through tribalism, thousands of their own citizens have died and their economy has been pauperized. They cannot blame oppression from outsiders or Marxist atheistic or Islamic plots against them. It puts the standing lie to the claim that Christians only need to change individuals in order to change society. Even Christian mission societies see the Ugandan Church as a hopeless cause.

Will their God-talk have any power or relevance, except an emotional sense that in the midst of those struggles they have held on bravely? But their perseverance is not the issue. The issue is that in spite of being Christian people, they have messed their situation up. Where they should have proved the power of the gospel to bring a transformation of society, they have failed to do so. The Church needs to think very carefully through its very understanding of God-talk in its own situation. Otherwise, the power of tribalism to divide appears to be greater than the power of Christ to unite. The God of the Bible, the God and Father of Jesus Christ, has not brought about the kind of transformation that the Scriptures seem to claim he offers. What kind of a God, or what kind of an understanding is possible in such a situation? Unfortunately, that kind of a challenge was not raised at Lambeth. But it needs to be made. For if, as Gutierrez claims, God is a God who in involvement with the context focuses especially on the poor, where is, or has been, the God of Ugandan Christians?

The nature of revelation

One position represented at the Conference saw the answer to the question of God-talk in the givenness of revelation. This view held that the Bible has a quality and authority not granted to any other scriptures. Theology is contained in the apostolic interpretations of the text. Exponents of this view were Bishop Graham Leonard of London and Archbishop Donald Robinson of Sydney. The givenness of revelation rises above every context. What the apostles defined as a basic imperative for the Church in their own context rises as it stands above every other context. This view was most relevant in the discussion on the ordination of women, where the apostle Paul's interpretation of Scripture was a key issue in the debate.

Bishop Leonard argued that there were two different assumptions about revelation and culture: 'If you believe that the pattern and structure of creation within which God has given us the freedom to love and serve him, a pattern and structure which includes the creation of humanity as male and female is to be minimized and as far as possible ignored; that the place and culture of the incarnation are of no abiding significance; that in choosing twelve men to be his apostles our Lord was simply moved by cultural conditioning; that Holy Orders are not appointed by Divine Providence; that Scripture and tradition have lost their authority and that all decisions in Church matters must be made in the light of "appropriateness" and "expediency"; that the language and images in which God has chosen to speak about himself and in which he bids us speak of him can be modified or discarded; that, in the words of one bishop, "every assertion that Christianity in any form possesses by divine revelation the ultimate and unchanging truth will have to be abandoned"; that the revelation given in Christ needs to be modified to suit modern man. . . . What they represent is not the Eternal Gospel which the Church has proclaimed for nearly two thousand years. When we try to discuss the specific problems relating to the ordination of women to the priesthood, these attitudes keep cropping up, so making discussion difficult because we start with different assumptions particularly about revelation and culture.'

Bishop Leonard's argument suggests a view of revelation which lifts it above cultural conditioning. He described his own view as follows: 'God spoke and acted uniquely in Christ and—and I quote—"Holy Scripture is the unique record of the nature and activity of God and of God's purpose for his people . . . having an authority and authoritativeness which must have no rival in its control over us if the Church is to continue to be the community, sign and servant of God's salvation for this world".'

Archbishop Donald Robinson of Sydney put forward a motion calling for dioceses not to go ahead with the ordination of women. He held it to be contrary to the explicit teaching of the New Testament that women should be given responsibility for the authoritative and regulative ministry of God's word in the congregation, that ministry which is at the heart of the pastoral office of bishop and presbyter. He considered it to be wrong for the Anglican Church to depart from Scripture, especially where that Scripture had been endorsed by the unvarying tradition of the Church. His section of the Conference had been speaking much of Scripture and tradition as the two primary criteria of authority. He wanted to dissuade his fellow bishops from so fundamental a departure from scriptural, apostolic and catholic faith and order.

Some 40 per cent of the bishops supported him. Archbishop Robinson told us in an interview that it seemed to him that: 'we never even came near any common mind as to how the Bible is to be handled as an application. We were full of formulas about tradition and reason and both of which have to be bent around now. There is no content in tradition any more; tradition is what you do day by day. Reason is what is reasonable in any given culture at any given time. Although the dominion of Scripture is proclaimed formally and I think quite sincerely, it has got no room to move and get the edge on either tradition or reason, in the way it did in the Reformation. There is very little sign of Scripture shifting anything in the present debate.'

Archbishop Robinson told us that he thought that in his plenary presentation Rowan Williams tried to jump directly from his argument that Jesus comes to liberate and free, to the situations that need solutions. The presentation had an apostle-shaped gap, moving from the liberating Christ, as long as what happened appears to be liberating somebody. Everything is referable to whether or not it has a certain experiential impact.

He continued: 'There are some relativities related to our cultures. You must talk in language, which is a cultural thing. You must avoid things which simply put up great barriers of communication. I do not know what to do beyond that to be quite honest, and I think I rather warmed to the David Gitari line that there are some things you affirm and some things you will not know and some things on which you will be neutral. ... But you cannot arrive at anything very useful by the method we have adopted here.'

A contrary view was represented by Elizabeth Templeton, from the Presbyterian Church of Scotland, in her response to the Archbishop of Canterbury's keynote address on unity. Her speech had finely drawn features and a sharp humour. For her, the

givenness of revelation was irrelevant. It is impossible to rise above
the context we are in. The only certainty is risk. The mark of
authentic revelation that brings change is risk.

She observed that one central theological question, deeply
embedded in all the internal and ecumenical debates about authority, is what level of provisionality we can properly live with
together, under a God who is for us, ahead of us, not within our
grasp. This was the hardest underlying polarity in inter-denomi-
national and intra-denominational battles.

She identified that some believed that the invincibility of God's
love discloses itself in some kind of absolute safeguarded articulation, whether of Scripture, Church, tradition, clerical line-
management, agreed reason, charismatic gifts, orthopraxis—or any
combination of such elements. While others believed that the
invincibility of God's love discloses itself in the relativity and risk
of all doctrine, exegesis, ethics, piety and ecclesiastical structure,
which are the Church's serious exploratory play, and which exist at
an unspecifiable distance from the face to face truth of God.

She therefore asked: 'What unity is possible in concrete existence between those on either side of the trans-denominational
divide seems to me our toughest ecumenical question. If we can
find a way through that one, I suspect that all our specific problems
of doctrine, ministry and authority will come away as easily as
afterbirth. But if we seek in any of our bilateral or multilateral
shifts to mask, suppress or smother that divide, our so-called unity
will be a disastrous untruth.'

After Elizabeth Templeton's presentation, we had two different
reactions from the same country. One archbishop commented on
her brilliant theological analysis. But one bishop, who was a
consultant, thought that her speech was many fine things, but not
theology.

The theological importance of risk is identified by the Indian
ecumenical theologian M.M. Thomas.[2] For him, bringing transformation in any context is such a dominating passion that in some
cases it may mean risking Christ himself in order that the Kingdom of Christ is born among people. There are no boundaries to
this risking of Christ. Everything accepted as given must be placed
at risk.

Rowan Williams in his response to a presentation on authority
by Archbishop Keith Rayner, looked at the nature of Jesus'
authority in the Gospels. Certainty is not to be found in the words

but in actions. For Williams, the authority of revelation is in what conserves and witnesses to the authority of Jesus in setting the world free from sin and diabolical bondage.

He noted that Jesus' teaching was characterized by 'authority' (Matt. 7.29; Mark 1.22; Luke 4.32,36); but this is not comparable to the 'authority' that settles disputes or provides definitive information. Judging from the vocabulary of the Gospels, it is bound up with the decisive effectiveness of what Jesus *does*. Authority is shown in the forgiveness of sins, in power over unclean spirits, in the sovereign liberty to heal, to set free, to act for God. The idea of authority in the Gospels is connected far more with how we do things than with how we know things.

He therefore argued that the givenness of the gospel is integrally related to the action of Jesus in the gospel, setting the world free from sin and diabolical bondage. To ask about the Christian authorization for this or that practice, this or that doctrine, is to ask how it relates to the promise of becoming a child of God, how it serves the disciple's task of proclaiming and effecting the offer of new life in the Kingdom. The status of teaching about the divinity of Christ, the Trinity, the Scriptures and the sacraments must be rooted in this matter of their relatedness to this new life.

He therefore urged caution about assuming uncritically that we already know what is essential for the preaching of the gospel, or that we might be able to come up with a criterion of authoritativeness independent of the living out of our mission, the effort to make real in the world the promise of decisive forgiveness and renewal.

He concluded that: 'In the Church's life, we are not to look for a criterion of authority divorced from the pattern of lives transformed; and a Church which could claim impeccable credentials for imparting authoritative information about the sources of the Christian enterprise, but had no capacity to speak or act with conviction for the sake of the world's liberation would not be sharing in the *exousia* of Jesus.'

For many mission theologians from the Two Thirds World, the givenness of the gospel is not in question. But the key to understanding the gospel is the enfleshment of the gospel in the incarnation of our Lord. So incarnation is the starting point of theological content and method. The incarnation is a key to the method of understanding revelation and doing theology. To interpret Scripture, we therefore need first to be involved in our own context with the stances of Jesus, especially his stances with relation to the little people of the earth, the poor, the sinners, the outcastes of society, and not the self-righteous; then to ask questions of the text of Scripture that arise from our context; to allow the Scripture then to speak with relevance to the context and in turn to challenge the context and our questions. With these questions from Scripture, we then continue our involvement in our context and bring new questions to Scripture. This is a process described by some as 'the hermeneutical circle'. It is a method originated by theologians from the Two Thirds World who have been impressed by the sociological point that every interpreter of Scripture is influenced by his or her own sociological position. The women's presentation at Lambeth argued this point forcefully in terms of patriarchal understandings of God. Bishops David Gitari, Henry Okullu and Peter Hatendi all expressed the outworkings of this procedure in their presentations.

This method differs from a process known as indigenization, which is to take an already formulated set of propositions about the teaching of Scripture and then seek to clothe them in concepts and illustrations taken from a particular culture. Such a method is as far as the view of Bishops Leonard and Robinson can go in relating Scripture to individual cultures.

What God-talk requires

Gustavo Gutierrez gave an eloquent and simple model of this way of relating the text and the context. Speaking from a context where the theology of liberation dominates, he stressed that God-talk first required contemplation, worship and prayer.

Contemplation, worship and prayer

He stated: 'In order to speak on God, in order to do theology, we need first to contemplate God. Contemplation, worship, prayer is an essential dimension of all Christian life. We must accept the gift of the gratuitous love of God. At the same time we must put in practice the will of God. Contemplation and commitment are the two essential aspects of any Christian life. Without contemplation, we have not begun; nor without commitment to all persons in the situations of the last ones. Only after we enter together into contemplation and commitment, we call this praxis. Theology is a reflection on praxis in the light of faith. We are bound to these two aspects, contemplation, prayer and commitment. Only afterwards is it possible to do theology—to speak on God.

'The first moment is the moment of silence. The second moment is the moment of speaking. This distinction between these two moments in our doing theology is basically very classic. St Anselm of Canterbury said *"Credo ut intellegam"*—"I am not trying to understand in order to believe, but I believe in order to understand." Christian theology is a reflection about living faith.

'One consequence for our response is to follow Jesus Christ. In the gospel he said, "Go into the world to make disciples of all nations." He did not say "Go into the world to do theology".'

The place of the poor in God-talk

Secondly, he drew attention to the nature of poverty and its role in God-talk today. He recalled that poverty was not only an economic, social or political reality. There was the tendency to see poverty only in the context of social questions. Poverty is a massive fact today in humanity. It is not new as a fact or a reality. But our consciousness today is different from in the past because the poor are more present in the history of humanity today. New nations in Africa, or old nations which are independent today in Asia, or the new presence of races of black people, all the oppressed persons, all women, are expressions of the new presence coming from an old reality.

For Gutierrez, poverty in the final analysis means death. Those who are close to the poor see this very well. While poverty has economic, social and political aspects, it is a physical death. People die through hunger and sickness and other kinds of poverty. It is spiritual death at the same time. Anthropologists like to say culture is life. The true poverty today in the world is the destruction of individuals, cultures, nations. We must be very conscious of these cold facts. Poverty is unjust and early death. He cited one Christian community from Haiti, one of the poorest countries in the world, and in his own continent, who said: 'Wherever we look we see death.' In Peru, he remembered very well a meeting of a basic Christian community and one old lady affirming, 'We, old persons, are close to death.' And a young lady there said, 'No, Grand-mother, today in Peru children are closer to death.'

He continued: 'When we speak about death we try to keep this cruel reality in mind: this is poverty. We must be not only conscious about this reality but at the same time conscious about the causes of poverty.

'We have not only death present in poverty. We can speak about a world of the poor. The poor belong to a race, a social class, a culture, but we can say that the poor belong to a world.'

Poverty means insignificance

Gutierrez said: 'The poor are the insignificant, not relevant persons. Let me give an example. In Latin America we are in a very painful situation. We have many cases of people missing. We remember very well the names of important persons who were killed—for example we remember very well the name of Bishop Romero, so important for our continent but also for all Christians. But we do not remember the names of poor persons who were killed. Even in death they are not significant. And for poor persons, their names are not significant. We know figures. For example, at the funeral of Bishop Romero, fifty persons were killed, but we do not know their names. The poor are present through figures, not through names.'

For Gutierrez, the poor are persons. To be poor is a way to know, a way to make friends, to love, to speak, to believe. He would not try to be balanced in his affirmations about these deep deprivations of our first right as persons and children of God—to live. The poor have many values. We may not start from deprivations. We must start from the cultural, personal and religious values of the poor. To be Christian is to enter into the world of the poor. We are not committed to the poor if we are committed to a culture, a race, a discriminated sex or a social class. We are committed to the poor if we have friends among poor persons. This is not an attempt to take a romantic way in order to speak about the poor. To have friends among the poor is to share our life with them and to consider them our equals. Love is possible only between equals. We may have compassion, but not love. We think we have nothing to receive from them. We are only to give to them.

Preferential option for the poor

Gutierrez continued: 'We speak today about the preferential
option for the poor. What is the ultimate reason for this preferential option. It is not our social analysis. A social analysis can be
useful to know the concrete situation in which a poor person is, but
it is not our ultimate reason for this commitment. It is not our
human compassion, though it is very important. Human compassion is not a last reason for this commitment. My own experience
of relative poverty in Latin America is not the reason. Often when
speaking in Europe or the United States, people tell me that I
speak on behalf of the poor because I am Latin American. My
main reason for talking about the poor and commitment to them is
because I am trying to be Christian. God is the ultimate reason for
this commitment.

'I come from a poor country. I live among poor in my city. I
cannot say all poor are good. We must be committed to the poor
not because the poor are good, but because God is good. Because
God is good, God prefers the last in the world and in our history.
We must try to love all persons, and especially the poor. No one is
outside the love of God. To love everyone, especially the last, the
basis for this is God. The gospel is not a revelation about the poor,
it is a revelation about God. Bless the poor because God is God is
the main idea of the Beatitudes—after that we must understand the
concrete situation of the poor.'

The language of justice

Gutierrez said: 'My third point is about speaking about God.
Every theology is a language about God. Today, what is the
appropriate language in order to say to the suffering people, the
innocent persons, "God loves you" ? I think we have maybe two
big ways in order to say this. One (I take this idea from the Book of
Job) is prophetic language. That is to say, to speak from God in
the place of and to insist on the place of the last in history, the
insignificant, the oppressed people. One aspect of this prophetic
language is justice. We cannot today speak on God without
reference to social injustice and by consequence about the con-
struction of a just world. Justice, prophecy is a language. . . . Our

language must be prophetic, announcing a life in a reality marked by death.'

The language of contemplation

Gutierrez affirmed: 'At the same time the other way in the Book of Job is this—is for a contemplative language. The content of this contemplative language is the most important and deepest point in the Bible—the gratuitous love of God. First in the Bible is the love of God. Our own actions are only answers to this first step coming from God. The gratuitous love of God is a big message of the Book of Job. We must place our requirements for justice in the context of the gratuitous love of God. The experience of all the persons working together among the poor is that to look only for justice can be inhuman. The struggle for justice needs to be placed in the context of the gratuitous love of God.

'To pray is an experience of gratuitousness. Because I try to be committed to the poor, I try to be sensitive. To meet especially the poor is to meet God. To meet God in our failure is a way to orthopraxis as well.'

Grounded in gratuitous love

Gutierrez declared: 'Our deepest aspiration as human beings is to be loved gratuitously. This is easy to understand because we were made in gratuitousness. For this reason we do not like to be loved by our merits. We want to be loved gratuitously because this is the beginning for us as human persons. The poor are very sensitive to gratuitous love. How to keep together these two dimensions of justice and contemplative language. From the poor countries in the world today a new contemplative language is being born. We must pay attention to these new languages. I think we have here something very profound and challenging to us.

'In conclusion. What is difficult for us, is to accept the presence of God in our history. One popular French poet has composed a poem beginning: "Our Father who art in heaven, stay there." This is the prayer of many people. Sometimes it is our prayer as well because the presence of God in our lives is disturbing us. It is a demanding presence. We prefer to believe in God, but far. Please we are so busy here, we have so many things to do. I think in the letter of St James we have twice one Greek word, *dipsuchos.* Literally it means you must avoid having two souls. This is a danger to have two souls in our life—one to believe in God, the other to do our own will. I say this because I think the only one way to understand our commitment to the poor is to accept God in our lives. This is the only one way for the Christian. This is a big danger for many of us to try to live two lives—one more or less Christian which are our affirmations to Christ and the other rebuking Jesus when he speaks about the price to pay.

Language of a community

Gutierrez concluded: ' I think today in our Churches, because to be Christian is to belong to a Christian community, to do theology is not an individual function. We must not try to do theology to write books. To do theology is an ecclesial function. It is in service of the Christian community. In the Church we have found Jesus Christ. His face has changed our lives. To do theology today means to be present in this Christian community, ecclesia, Church, and at the same time to look not only to the presence of the poor outside the Church. We have today many poor in the Christian churches.'

After this speech, the Archbishop of Canterbury commented that a former student of his had heard Gustavo Gutierrez lecture, and had said, 'After many years of study, at last I knew what theology was all about.'

Gustavo Gutierrez contributes to the question of God-talk in a significant way by identifying the following elements of authentic God-talk. There was first the contemplative stance: the realization that God has already taken hold of you. God-talk is a response to God. It is not possible to talk about God without having experienced God, and without responding to the gratuitous love of God.

Second, there is the prophetic stance. It is not possible to talk about God without taking a stance with relation to those who are suffering; or without recognizing that he is present and active in history. It is historically that we talk about God. This entails taking the context seriously.

He points out that among the poor, God-talk is giving birth to a new and profound language which must be listened to. It is grounded in the gratuitous given love of God, and so clearly related to the apostolic formulation that Bishops Leonard and

Robinson are so committed to. It is grounded in the same context as the apostles themselves spoke from; which one of the apostles was ever a rich man? It is a language about God that is grounded in worship, prayer and justice. It is a language not of individual rational certainties but of a community's experience.

Risking Christ

How does Gutierrez's thought contribute to the discussion on risk which Elizabeth Templeton raised, and which is explored by M.M. Thomas in his book *Risking Christ for Christ's Sake*. The question fundamentally is this. Some are willing to risk everything for the sake of the context. The context is so dominant in their thinking and concerns that they will risk anything to change the context. This is true for some liberation theologians struggling against social oppression, and for theologians of dialogue with Asian religions. No boundaries are allowed in seeking to relate to and change the context. Even for some, the uniqueness of Christ does not present a boundary. They will even risk Christ for the sake of the context. To risk Christ for the sake of Christ actually collapses into risking Christ for the sake of the context. This is where the initially helpful insight that sociological considerations influence the perspective of the interpreters of Scripture, collapses into the Marxist dogma that all philosophy and religion is 'the heart of a heartless world' and has no objective truth in it.

At the end of the day, risking Christ for the context results in losing Christ for the sake of the context. A Christ who does not make any real difference to the context is no Christ; he is an idol. What right has any Christian to risk Christ; for Christ is the one who has helped shape you so that you can understand and deal with the context.

In sharp contrast, the Africans were adamant that everything is to be risked, even a tolerable life itself for the sake of Christ. They would rather bear the suffering and ambiguities of their context, its poverty, religious intolerance, and social injustice and yet cling to Christ. They look to Christ alone to transform their context. They apply Christ, but they do not risk him.

The contribution of Gustavo Gutierrez is to point out that authentic and biblical God-talk is a language that is ready to risk anything except Christ. Jesus himself said that the poor were blessed because the Kingdom was theirs. He is already among the poor. So in being involved with the poor, one never risks losing Christ, for he is there with them. In the context of the poor, it is not possible to take the context without Christ or Christ without the context.

The only appropriate way of risking Christ is the way such people as Gutierrez have demonstrated, both in praxis and in concept; namely, risking conceptual formulations, recognizing that the focus of God-talk in the Scripture is towards the poor, in loving, sharing and incarnating in that direction. In such a context, risking Christ is only to find him.

The issue finally becomes an issue of the authority of Scripture. The issue of authority in the Anglican Communion held the Conference's attention throughout, and it is to this that we now turn.

Notes

1. Lamin Sanneh: distinguished Ghanaian professor of mission and author of *West African Christianity* (Maryknoll, Orbis, 1983).
2. M.M.Thomas *Risking Christ for Christ's Sake* (Geneva, World Council of Churches, 1987).

CHAPTER 8

Authority in the Church

The Conference devoted considerable time in its plenary presentations and discussion to the question of authority in the Church.

Questions of authority

There is the question of the authority of revelation. Gustavo Gutierrez identified that the question which raises the issue of authority in the West is how do we speak of God in a world where God seems unnecessary.

A.T. and R.P.C. Hanson, in *The Identity of the Church,*[1] distinguish the question of authority *in* the Church from the question of the authority *of* the Church. Is authority in the Church exercised because of office held or because of competence shown? An example of authority resting on office is the Roman Catholic notion that authority is vested in the Pope, bishops and priests. Anglican structures of authority tend to become juridical and institutional instead of charismatic and pastoral.

How is authority understood in the Anglican Communion? The bishops from the Two Thirds World came into a context where there is a tradition of an understanding of authority of which they too are a part. What is that tradition, and what are they bringing to it?

Plural sources of authority

The sources of authority according to the 1948 Lambeth Conference are Scripture, tradition, creeds, the ministry, the witness of the saints and the *sensus fidelium*. The ARCIC Final Report spoke of the authority of the ordained ministry, not merely a delegated function but sacramental and inherent. Authority is both singular, in that it derives from the mystery of the divine Trinity, and plural, in that it is distributed in numerous organically related elements, describing the data, ordering them, and mediating and verifying them. The plurality of sources disperses authority, recognizes conflict between them, and checks against the temptation to tyranny and unhampered power. The crucible in which these elements of authority are fused is liturgy.[2]

The traditional understanding of authority dispersed in Scripture, reason and tradition is the given in the way the Two Thirds World Church understands authority. This understanding has been taught, received and, especially in the case of Scripture, rarely questioned. It has coexisted with a variety of ways in which religious authority is understood and experienced in the Two Thirds World context.

In Asia, the authority of religion and tradition includes the whole of life. It is not expressed primarily in faith commitments and formulations, but in a whole way of life. Many Christians in Asia live in a context where other religions have sacred scriptures, to which their adherents give the same degree of authority as Christians accord to the Bible.

South Asian Christians also have an experience of democratization in the Church with their practice of Bishops in Council. The Diocesan Councils and Synods are the ruling body of the Church where the overwhelming majority are laity. The bishop has a role as guardian of the faith. But no decision in matters of faith and order can be made without the full participation of the laity who include women. This is in harmony with the Anglican understanding of authority dispersed in a plurality of sources. But it is not a case of theology by democracy. It is the recognition that the people of God as a whole have a central role in the exercise of authority.

The African understanding of authority is normally vested in traditional leaders like chiefs and elders. In many societies political and religious authority are both vested in the same person. Again, authority is not primarily a matter of faith formulations but actions in the community of those vested with authority.

This is the necessary background to examining the discussion of the threefold sources of authority in the Anglican Communion.

The authority of Scripture

The place of the very sources of authority is being questioned in the communion. In the North the issue is the place of Scripture; in the South, where Scripture still has a supreme place, the question is its interpretation.

The authority of Scripture refers to its unique and reliable witness to the foundation events of the Church's faith. Scripture is not just a reporter reporting, but an interpreter responding.

Is Scripture to be interpreted according to its plain sense? The plain sense signifies that the meaning is clear, is supra-cultural, and can be applied to all cultures. Our starting point is our present historical and cultural situation. Reason is widely accepted as the neutral, trustworthy faculty which can objectively work on the plain sense of Scripture. We make sense for ourselves today. Making sense is not reducible to a single method. A physicist seeks sense. Social and political thinkers use other categories. All seek consistency and integrity, arguing, persuading and coming to conclusions. Making sense is as flawed and limited as the rest of human activity.

Tradition

Tradition is the history of reading the Scriptures. Others have been here. The Church and believers have been here. In *Stepping Stones*, James Atkinson and Rowan Williams write, 'If the Bible shows what it is like to be converted by God's interrupting of the world, the history of the faithful reading of the Bible shows what it means for the converted speech of Scripture to be also converting speech for generations after.' 'Tradition represents the critical spirit of the Church, made acute by the Holy Spirit; a creative recovery of the past in the context of an idle, banal or corrupt present. . . . One distinctive insight of a Reformed theology is that tradition includes the memories of deep discontinuities.'[3] They argue that tradition is not a retreat into the past for answers. We need to view tradition as a conversation with the past, not a captive nor a capitulation to it.

Reason

Reason refers to the whole culture and context of logic, reason and reasoning. The dominant mode of reasoning is the gathering and piling up of evidence on one side or the other of an argument, laying bare one's presuppositions and framing a hypothesis. The scholar can then make a reasoned presentation. Others could respond that the evidence does not necessarily confirm the hypothesis or that the logic is inconsistent. This way of using reason opts for consistency. Reason means lack of excess, reasonableness and balance.

How are these sources perceived by the Two Thirds World?

What is the Two Thirds World's perception of these sources of authority? Scripture is authoritative, central and primary. In some areas, there is a very traditional view of the high authority of Scripture. In others, there are very radical views where the Old Testament is replaced by the scriptures of other religions. The real debate, however, lies in the area of interpretation.

Tradition

Tradition in the Two Thirds World Anglican churches has a number of referents. It does not primarily refer to the traditions of the first four councils and the fathers.

First, it refers to what is generally considered Anglican, what has always been done by Anglicans. It refers to the liturgical and ritual practices of eighteenth- and nineteenth-century Anglicanism, as first introduced into countries during the colonial expansion of the Anglican Church. As they came with the gospel and were part of the reception of the Christian faith, the same status was accorded to traditional practices as well as to traditional doctrinal formulations since both were taught and received. They were also frozen in time. Thus in Nigeria and Uganda the Anglican Church still uses the 1662 prayer book. Tradition is found in the worship forms and is equated with Anglican liturgical and pastoral practice.

The African bishops have a strong commitment to what they understand as Anglican tradition. At Lambeth they took strong, conservative and traditional stances on the issues of rights for homosexuals, women's ordination, evangelism, and relations with other religions. To some, their stances sounded obscurantist. But such was not the case. They fundamentally refused to accept an understanding of the development of doctrine which is prevalent in the Western Churches and is described by Reginald Fuller: 'We have already indicated that Anglicanism accepts the *Sola Scriptura* of the Reformation and that in the nuanced sense that only in Scripture do we find authoritative witness to the Christ event. We also note that Scripture has its centre in that witness but also that there are contingent applications of that witness to ongoing situations in the New Testament period. This resulted in developments in the understanding of the original biblical witness and consequently in doctrinal development or trajectories.'[4]

Such suspicion of other forms of tradition in the Two Thirds World comes from the evangelical origin and foundation of many of their churches. The supreme authority of Scripture in theology meant that tradition hardly had any place as a basis for authority. It was reduced to and confused with Anglican liturgical practice and the thirty-nine articles. But evangelicalism itself was a tradition. Their dismissal of tradition meant that these churches grew up without a clear understanding of the role of tradition in authority in the Church. They saw tradition as a question of liturgical correctness, not theological correctness. This means that if the Archbishop of Canterbury, the Lambeth Conference or the English Church practises these things, they become right.

Tradition is often equated with liturgy, with the use of robes, stole or scarf, and the place of the table or altar. It cannot be altered because of the high view of Scripture and the suspicion of the development of doctrine, and therefore of any development of tradition (as we will note later in the chapter). So African Churches have not really made a mark on the development of tradition, as they felt they did not need to.

This use of tradition in their churches often stifles the kind of free worship which reflects local culture, and which is desperately trying to break out in Anglican congregations. Such worship is often seen as not being Anglican. The real leaders of this worship are the lay people. The pastor is often on the sidelines for he is trained in Anglican, not cultural, practices. He does not do things which are not quite Anglican.

The second referent of tradition is the religious traditions of their own fathers, the traditions of their cultures. The vigil is an African religious tradition. In the religious cultures of Africa and Asia, these traditions were wholly bound up with non-Christian religions and were, for that reason, rejected by the churches. For example, outcaste Indian converts did not want to be reminded of religious traditions from Hindu culture which spoke to them of their untouchable status. This view still obtains in parts of the Anglican Communion. As noted earlier, a holy table with a dragon on it was recently destroyed in Singapore Cathedral, because of its supposed demonic associations.

With the coming of independence to the South Asian countries and United Churches, there was a move to develop the national identity of the churches by trying to incorporate the traditions of their own cultures into the life and worship of the Church. If Western Christians could use pagan fir trees to celebrate the gift of eternal life in Jesus, and the pagan custom of having bridesmaids at weddings to confuse the malevolent spirits as to who was the bride, then Indian Christians could incorporate into their liturgy a ceremony for blessing a house.

Unfortunately, this aspect of the role of tradition was not discussed at Lambeth. The Western understanding of tradition as the theological tradition of the fathers still dominates the corporate consciousness of the Anglican Communion when it talks about tradition. The South Asian bishops could have made a significant contribution to the African churches in this area, especially in wrestling with the theological questions raised by using traditions from contexts where non-Christian religions are dominant. It is in this context that the all-night vigil at Lambeth must be understood. A vigil was held on Thursday, 28 July, called by the African bishops and led by Archbishop Tutu to express solidarity with suffering people throughout the world. Africans normally keep vigils when someone dies, and observe them the night before a burial service. A vigil is not considered Anglican in many parts of Africa. The fact that a vigil was held at Lambeth gives affirmation to this African religious tradition. The Africans have a desperate urge to relate to their own traditions. Archbishop Browne saw the vigil as a contribution of African culture to the life of the Church. As a result of Lambeth, African pastors will now be involved in vigils which have now become a part of the tradition and so can be accepted as traditional in their terms. But the Anglican Communion needs to recognize that tradition means not only the first four centuries of doctrinal tradition. Two Thirds World provinces must develop their own practices that are culturally compatible. The communion as a whole must move to see that those practices can become traditional. In the same way as these other practices from England have become their tradition, so their own cultural practices can become a tradition and be made available to the rest of the Church.

Ethics

The Africans held on to tradition in the midst of tremendous theological pressures. In a debate on homosexual rights, Bishop Paul Moore from New York put forward the view that homosexual tendencies were a matter of chemical imbalance and therefore not a suitable subject for praise or blame. He proposed a motion that: 'This Conference: 1) reaffirms the Statement of the Lambeth Conference of 1978 on homosexuality, recognizing the continuing need in the next decade for a "deep and dispassionate study of the question of homosexuality, which would take seriously both the teaching of scripture and the results of scientific and medical research"; 2) urges such study and reflection to take account of biological, genetic and psychological research being undertaken by other agencies, and the socio-cultural factors that lead to the different attitudes in the Provinces of our Communion also deserve further study; 3) calls each Province to work toward the elimination of discrimination against homosexual persons in the Church and in the world and to support their human rights.'

Here was a bishop from the West allowing the context of scientific investigation to be so totally dominant that the context began to dictate in advance what was to be believed. Bishop Moore was prepared to accept the judgement of scientists over and against a biblical judgement. This process may be the result of accepting a kind of development of doctrine which holds that science holds the key to all mysteries.

Bishop Michael Nazir-Ali from Pakistan felt that the Conference was saved in the nick of time from saying unwise things about homosexuality that could not be proved. Archbishop Manasses Kuria attributed the opposition of the Africans to the motion to their understanding of morality: 'Homosexuals have rights as human beings. But they do not have rights as homosexuals. Homsexuality is sin. We do not call homosexuals to be faithful in marriage to one another. That is to call sin holy. There would also be a contradiction of our desire to restrict the spread of AIDS if we condoned homosexual behaviour.'

In making their stand, the Africans were implicitly stressing that ethics is also a criterion of truth; that truth cannot escape morality. Ethics is central to being human in the world. So any Scripture has to be read in relation to ethical imperatives. It is not just reason that enables us to discover what the word of God is. Since Scripture has to do with us as people, it has to do not only with our mind but also with our ethical life.

Experience

So Scripture, tradition understood as the Church's theological tradition, and reason are not a total description of the sources of authority in the Anglican Communion. To them must be added morality. Experience must be added as well. In the Two Thirds World, reason cannot be separated from experience. Bishop Bashir Jeevan's presentation showed dependence on arguing from what works in his context. The whole emphasis on theology in context, stressed by Gustavo Gutierrez and the women's presentation, focuses on experience—as does the charismatic movement in the West. Two Thirds World people are giving an authority to experience in their theological formulations. The final report indicates this in the section on Social Order. 'There is also a short-term aspect to tradition, perhaps better described as "experience". Part of the basis for authentic Christian response to social issues has to lie in acknowledging the validity of first-hand experience, the living witness of those actually engaged in the issues under discussion' (section 27).

Reason

The Conference appeared to be divided on the place given to reason. The final report on Dogmatic and Pastoral Concerns identifies reason as a cultural phenomenon: 'The pressures of grassroots evangelism and the renewing power of charismatic movements are a reminder that Western rationalism is also in many respects a "local culture" that programmes out those things that are uncomfortable'(section 38). By contrast, the report on Christianity and the Social Order suggests that, 'the reasoning mind needs to assert that there is an ultimate truth towards which all our valid but partial knowledge converges' (section 30).

Reason is not only an individual activity—it is also a communal activity. We reason together. Reason is not just a question of an individual sitting down and laying out a position logically. It is what seems reasonable to a group of people. Africans accept something because it seems reasonable to the whole group. The final report on Dogmatic and Pastoral Concerns makes this point: 'Reason means not so much the *capacity* to make sense of things as it does "that which makes sense" or "that which is reasonable". The appeal to reason then becomes an appeal to what people—and that means people in a given time and place—take as good sense or "common" sense. It refers, in short, to what we can call the "mind" of a particular culture, with its characteristic ways of seeing things, asking about them, and explaining them' (section 82).

Consensus means what is reasonable. Homosexuality cannot be shown to be reasonable. When women's ordination and homosexuality are shown to be commonly acceptable, Africans will accept them. Since at the moment everybody is happy, there is no reason to change. If discontent cannot be handled, it has to be incorporated and drained of bitterness. Then a consensus will come and will be accepted.

Moses Tay from Singapore shows a similar concern for consensus and contentment in resisting the process of injecting false division and conflict into the process of the Conference. He was particularly concerned at what he saw as a spirit of discontent, of always being anti-this or anti-that, which tended to make people unhappy. 'Godliness with contentment is great gain but sometimes the Church wants to inject discontent and anti-attitudes. If people know the Lord, why are they so unhappy? I think such a spirit of discontent is not from the Lord. If it is allowed into the Church, it divides the Church.'

What would have happened if the discussion on the ordination of women had taken into account these various factors in Anglican tradition as they are actually practised? The debate was between people who were arguing across a divide on the nature of revelation, but who were united in accepting the primacy of reason. That road led to an impasse so they ended up with a pragmatic compromise based on experience and expediency. Had they asked the various regional groups to meet by themselves and make their regional contributions, we suggest that the Africans would have said that firstly, Scripture neither rejects nor commands the ordination of women. So there is freedom to think it through.

Second, it leaves room to look at our traditions very carefully in the light of Scripture, and to relate Scripture to our traditions and to see them as God-given as well. Thirdly, we may consult our experience. We suggest that it was from this basis that the Africans at Lambeth made the contribution that pragmatically it was not the right time for them to proceed with such ordinations.

Reason—consistency or consensus

In the Two Thirds World, reason is found in consensus alongside of consistency in logic. Consistent logic is important to those who are educated and trained. But the dominant structure of reason is the consensus of a group of people who have considered the issue. Its mode is more relational than logical: whether people accept a proposition is more to the fore than the actual content of the proposition.

But consensus can produce oppression. In Uganda many bishops welcomed Idi Amin's *coup d'etat*. But eventually Archbishop Janani Luwum was willing to take on the government. In Germany, the Churches accepted Hitler by consensus for a long time.

The Church has contained a prophetic element which takes the evidence, and has the prophetic concern to push for change. But prophetic logical reasoning which goes in the direction it leads whatever happens, is not dominant in the Two Thirds World. The dominant reasoning is consensus: 'we will believe and understand together'. That is why the Two Thirds World Churches produce statements but not famous individual theologians. They are closer to the understanding of *Credo ut intellegam* than to a tradition of tight, even arid, reasoning.

This shows the importance of the primates all getting together and deciding, rather than a universal primate making the decisions. At Lambeth, the African bishops were asking for a common theological statement which could be imposed on others, because for them it is not imposition, but arrival at a consensus that must be acceptable to all.

Bishop Charles Mwaigoga of Tanzania was one who wanted a decision from the Conference: 'I would be happy to see the Lambeth Conference come up with some decision that will be binding. I want something more than sharing one another's experiences. Anglicans are facing a problem. They want this freedom that means nobody has the authority to decide except individual provinces. Just consulting one another in this way is quite an expensive exercise. It just ends there and does not make any difference. If you come or not, tell us or do not tell us, it does not make any difference. The Church in Africa at least looks for someone to come up with a decision for them.'

Bishop John Walker of Washington shared this concern that Lambeth come to some decisions: 'I see a shift in terms of Third World participation, but not in terms of Third World influence. The last Lambeth Conference was structured in such a way that basically what we were going to do was have Bible Study and worship together and talk about some things. But no resolutions would emerge, and no action would be taken. Spontaneously in the middle of the Conference, in every section, there was an explosion and a demand for a reconsideration of the agenda. That demand came as much from people like Desmond Tutu as from anybody else. These bishops do care. They come all this distance to pray together. It's wonderful. But I can pray, sing hymns and have spiritual renewal with bishops in the United States. I did not come all this way to do that. I came here to focus on a world, what's happening in the world, and what we should say about the world. How do we address South Africa, Third World debt, the terrible poverty that exists, hunger, and the displacement of human beings all over the African continent?'

For many bishops in different ways, Lambeth decisions do matter. African bishops needed the platform of the communion to express their concerns. Archbishop George Browne of Liberia said: 'We are strengthened if we can go back and say that these are the views of the communion.' For Onell Soto from Venezuela, through the resolutions 'we are speaking clearly about a number of issues, racism, oppression, the foreign debt which is problem number one in Latin America. The Conference has given us backing in our ministry in this area and we can tell people that this is the consensus of the Anglican Communion.'

Therefore bishops from the Two Thirds World were quite surprised that the Conference could not say anything but insisted on the autonomy of the dioceses. Every African insisted on a statement. For them a theological or doctrinal statement is not one that has been so worked out that it is logically consistent and can stand the test of any kind of theological argument. When they present a doctrinal statement, they mean that, 'this is what we together have considered: we have taken all the evidence that we could bring. We have talked and argued about it and this is what we believe. Therefore it is reasonable to ask other people to accept this.' The African bishops were asking for such a statement.

The Western bishops were saying that a theological statement must not be vulnerable to attack. Because of their belief in the development of doctrine, a theological statement should also be open. It should show that all the doors have not been closed, and that further development is possible. So it ends up being pretty vague.

The Two Thirds World questions such vagueness. When consensus is reached on something, other people must accept it not as perfect but as reasonable. Two Thirds World bishops take seriously their leadership role as bishops who uphold the faith, and together come to reasonable conclusions. They do not look up to a scholar bishop, who because of his intellectual ability is able to produce a brilliant piece of theological work that is almost impregnable, and therefore provides the basis for a theological advance.

Once it is perceived that 'rationalism', which identifies reason with the true order of nature is a local culture, and that reason as consistent logic does not have the dominant role in theologizing, an important question must be addressed. What is the source of the boundaries for human behaviour in pluralistic societies and a pluralistic world? The appeal to God, superior culture and reason are ruled out. There is then a gap between the positive law of the state and human behaviour which used to be filled by appeals to God or reason. Now there is a vacuum. Some governments fill it with an appeal to self-interest, others with an appeal to the demands of the collective. There is a need to develop an authority for Christian social concerns from the activity of the kingdom as a mustard seed, and silent leaven within society bearing witness within a culture. The demise of reason marks the demise of the attempt to impose a Christian social order from above.

Reception

Lambeth highlighted that aspect of the development of doctrine, called reception, where the mind of the Church is established over a period of time. This arose in the context of the consecration of women to the episcopate. With what understanding of reception did the Two Thirds World bishops come to the debate?

To the Africans, reception often appears to mean that a doctrine should be compatible with, but not necessarily transform, a culture. Doctrine is received by people who are shaped by a certain culture. The reception is not a theological point. The culture makes room for it. A person's theological understanding grows with their openness to the culture.

What key factors in a community makes reception or rejection of a theological idea like women's ordination possible? Is it the theological maturity of the community, growing acceptance by usage, or independent cultural changes such as socio-economic and political factors that shape that culture? If all three are involved, which has priority? Cultural accommodation, especially in the Two Thirds World, dictates religious practice. Religious practice often has to do with a person's cultural acceptability. So we will examine the reception issue and the development of doctrine from the Two Thirds World viewpoint.

Two Thirds World churches find development of doctrine difficult to accept because for them religious truth is always given, not something that is constantly changing and developing. This is especially true of those in an Islamic context. That is why they say if the Bible says that homosexuality is sin, it is a sin. Churches do not expect to develop a doctrine of a Christian understanding of sexuality. The culture in which they live would have forced development of doctrine at a much faster pace. They have not forced it because, for example, in an Islamic context, there is no development of doctrine. Doctrine is given and only needs to be explained or applied.

Two Thirds World Christian leaders understand the development of doctrine, but are unwilling to accept a concept of which they are deeply suspicious. They come from non-Christian contexts where the development of doctrine might produce something that is not acceptable. This has taken place already in the context of African traditional religions. In one Nigerian denomination, some Anglicans have taken part with others in developing a church that accommodates the idea of polygamy using biblical material. This has resulted in a new denomination, whose faith scarcely resembles that of traditional Christianity.

The issue of polygamy raises the question of development of

doctrine. This is why a number of African bishops were concerned not to allow the baptism of the wives and children of polygamists, even though they recognized the importance of the issue in their culture. They wanted to make it very plain that the givenness of Scripture was not questioned. They hold that polygamy is biblically wrong. Those Africans who sought the change saw the issue not as doctrinal, but only as one of pastoral care. The Africans see that doctrine can be applied but not developed in such a way that it departs from the basics of the given biblical faith as they understand it.

The Africans' uncertainty and caution in relation to women's ordination was also based on the fear that it was a departure from Scripture and an adherence to religious truth as given in the Scripture. Archbishop Browne of Liberia told us, 'Culture is judged by Scripture no matter where it is.' For them, such ordination is not clearly taught in the Bible. They do not want to draw out implications or see a development from assured biblical truths.

On the other hand, some bishops from the United States were pushing the African bishops to accept the change in the directive on polygamists as a doctrinal and theological issue. If polygamy is accepted theologically, then there are no sexual norms. The secular reality and its sexual orientation become prescriptive for those in that situation. Other sexual norms cannot be imposed. The Africans saw the issue of polygamy as essentially a pastoral issue, not one of an imposition of, or liberation from, sexual norms. They made very certain therefore by their reaction that they were not talking about letting down the standards of the Bible. Their understanding of marriage from the Bible was given and authoritative. There was no development in it which would make it depart from the norms. For the Africans, therefore, the issue of Scripture as given is critically important. There is a tension with the concept of the development of doctrine which results in all kinds of new ways of looking at things. It was quite obvious at the Conference that Western and Two Thirds World Anglicans were travelling along parallel but separate paths.

Authority and reception

Does an understanding given to one part of the Church become an authoritative stance for the whole Church? Is there a developing authority which as it grows and is received, becomes authoritative for the whole Church? While a doctrine is being received, what kind of authority does it have and what attitude should be taken towards it? Is there a Gamalieline judgement saying, 'Let it be till God reveals otherwise if it is of God' and if so, what is its theological basis?

A judgement, which like Gamaliel's in the Book of Acts, waits on the outcome to see if something is of God, leads the whole matter of authority into a democratic acceptance. What instruments help people to monitor whether the democratic acceptance is taking place, so that it does not become manipulated in a media dominated culture as, we will see, some people suspected the ARCIC (Anglican-Roman Catholic International Commission) process had become? We should recognize the dominance and importance of the media in enabling the communication and in falsifying and tailoring truth. Can we believe that the reception process will be immune from all that? How may it be immunized? Will bishops be the only ones to receive the doctrine? And are they immune to being manipulated or misled in the reception process?

A case study of reception at Lambeth

An important illustration of the working of a process of reception took place in the debate on the report of the first Anglican–Roman Catholic International Commission. The resolution welcomed the agreed statements of ARCIC I and the first report of ARCIC II. In its explanatory note it recorded some comments from provinces, for example, 'While we respect continuing anxieties of some Anglicans in the areas of "sacrifice" and "presence", they do not appear to reflect the common mind of the Provincial responses, in which it was generally felt that the Elucidation of Eucharistic Doctrine was a helpful clarification and reassurance.'

Bishop Timothy Dudley-Smith was not satisfied with this explanatory note and moved the following amendment: 'while noting and respecting the continuing anxieties and conscientious convictions of many Anglicans unable to support this resolution, nevertheless ... ' He was grateful that the explanatory note attached to the motion freely acknowledges the misgivings of some Anglicans with the current reports of ARCIC and the process of their consideration and welcome. That explanatory note speaks of a considerable measure of consensus which must mean something short of unanimity, of a style and language not universally appropriate, of the need for clarification, the lack of South American representation, and some unanswered questions.

He drew attention to an open letter dated Easter 1988, which was sent to all bishops of the Anglican Communion, signed by over 500 Anglican evangelical leaders from thirty-five countries: 'I was glad to hear Bishop George Carey say that it was carefully considered in the section. I have to add, though, that no word of that consideration appears in the text of the motion before you. The arguments of this letter are seriously, charitably and theologically set out. I therefore want to ask the Conference to include my amendment since without it the text of this motion as it stands contains no hint whatever of the misgivings of this or other substantial body of loyal Anglican opinion. Without some such reference I believe you will cause needless dismay to those who already feel they are being marginalized and scarcely listened to, and you will give to others the impression that the Anglican Communion stands more unitedly behind the present ARCIC documents than is demonstrably the case. I hope therefore you will see your way in fairness to include this modest amendment, thinking back to our Bible Study this morning, it would be " a friendly act".'

Bishop Mark Santer of Birmingham, the co-chairman of ARCIC II, the successor to the commission whose work was under discussion, replied by recalling that the clear endorsement in the motion was based on the responses which had come from the Churches and provinces of the communion. The task of the Conference was to give expression and articulation together to the voices of the churches.

He continued: 'Of course there are some people who are not entirely happy with the way these agreed statements are expressed and who would have liked to have put it otherwise if they had been in the meeting. That is of the nature of such statements always and on all sides. And as we have been reminded, they have been expressed and they are explicitly recognised in the explanatory note which is appended to the resolution. But there is a distinction and an important one between the hesitations of individuals, however distinguished, and the mind of the Churches communally expressed. The mind of the Churches is quite clear. As the explanatory note says, the provinces gave a clear yes to the statement on eucharistic doctrine and the provinces gave a clear yes to the statement on ministry and ordination. And it is this positive judgement from our Churches and provinces which is what is expressed in the resolution.

'To put the hesitations of individuals into the main resolution, in the way proposed by Bishop Tim Dudley-Smith, would I think give a disproportionate and negative tone to our response which would not in fact correspond to the mind of our provinces as they have formally expressed it. I believe that Bishop Dudley-Smith's position is adequately and publicly covered by the explanatory note and I hope therefore that the Conference will reject his amendment and pass the resolution in the form proposed by the section on ecumenical relations. That is the kind of encouragement which we who are currently engaged in the dialogue on your behalf will appreciate as we continue our work on behalf of the Churches.'

It is significant to note the way in which the views of 500 leaders and the mind of the Church was contrasted. Bishop Santer said: 'There is a distinction, and an important one, between the hesitations of individuals, however distinguished, and the mind of the Churches communally expressed. The mind of the Churches is quite clear.' This was skilful use of a communication process to undermine the reception of a whole viewpoint. If people who may be a minority in a synod do not win the day, what are the means for their views to be heard by the communion, if they represent a number of minorities? Bishop Santer seemed to be using the weight of institutional processes to marginalize views which a significant number of responsible people felt needed to be expressed. Is this an exemplar of how the process of reception will be undertaken, for no other exemplar seems to exist at the moment?

Or will there be regular mass prayer meetings or 24-hour vigils to monitor whether the reception is taking place properly or not? Or will the media and the human communication process be given a sanctified status such that the human communication process is automatically going to bring about a reception that will reflect the mind of God? This is to invest the reception process with the very mind of God.

The African contribution of consensus is so important here because it takes into account the mind of minorities. No African could make the statement that Bishop Santer made that the EFAC (Evangelical Fellowship in the Anglican Communion) letter only reflected 500 individuals. An African leader would say: 'Those leaders are significant people, and represent a significant group of people and a significant view point—it must be included within what we finally come out with so that those people are also happy.' Whether they go through due process is irrelevant, because that due process is a marginalizing process.

The issue of decision-making

The discussion of authority ended up by eventually discussing the process of making authority work in discussing the instruments of decision-making. In several areas, the Conference never really resolved the issue of the dispersal of authority.

Notes

1. A.T. and R.P.C. Hanson, *The Identity of the Church* (London, SCM Press, 1987), ch. 8, 'The Authority of the Church', p. 190.
2. Stephen Sykes, 'Authority in Anglicanism', in Stephen Sykes, *The Identity of Anglicanism* (London, Mowbrays, 1978) pp. 87–88.
3. Rowan Williams and James Atkinson, 'On Doing Theology', in *Stepping Stones*, ed. by Christina Baxter (London, Hodder & Stoughton, 1987) p.10.
4. Reginald Fuller, 'Scripture', in Stephen Sykes and John Booty (eds), *The Study of Anglicanism* (London, SPCK, 1988), p. 88.

CHAPTER 9

Instruments of Communion

The real issue underlying the debate and process of developing instruments of decision-making was the issue of comprehensiveness and diversity—how the Anglican Communion could keep itself together in unity and yet allow diversity. There are four different factors in tension.

First, there is the concern for dispersed authority, which we noted in Chapter 8. The Anglican Communion is always suspicious of centralized authority. Lambeth '88 again saw the autonomy of the provinces stressed. This autonomy is important. The Anglican Communion is essentially focused on those who are symbols of unity in their own church. A bishop is a focus of unity because of the autonomous structure in which he is placed. A bishop cannot be such a focus of unity if he is dependent on someone else. In the relationship of bishops to one another a sense of unity is provided for the whole Church. If one focus of unity is needed among them, a universal primacy is possible but not necessary. Everyone at Lambeth relates out of strength because they bring their dioceses with them; they bring that which they represent and which defines them. So 'my diocese' and 'my people' is a legitimate expression because the bishop has become a corporate personality. Bringing their dioceses therefore gave them tremendous strength.

Secondly, this authority is dispersed in national churches. National churches, as we saw in Chapter 1, are an important feature and strength of the Anglican Communion. And national churches means there will always be a diversity of cultures and viewpoints.

Third, this diversity entails a commitment to comprehensiveness. And fourthly, there is a commitment to unity. In many ways, the Conference could have spelt disaster for the Anglican Communion. It was very English in style and tone. At the outset, people were very aware of their diversity, yet the communion held together. Indeed, as David Jenkins remarked to us at the end, euphoria seemed to be breaking out.

It did not hold together because of any magic formula of structural relationships. Structurally all the Church leaders are independent. Without any Pope there was a feeling of unity, because all Anglican bishops are symbols of unity in their autonomous structures. There is a genuine commitment to hold together come what may.

Bringing the diocese was an important aspect of sharing the unity. The bishops realised how the Church is the Church of God because they saw the Spirit working in a marvellous and wonderful variety of ways. When they saw the diocese and not the bishop, then the caricatures began to melt and they began to say, 'We are learning something'.

Is the unity of the Anglican Communion for the sake of holding things together, or is it a unity that facilitates new identities to develop? The struggle of the Two Thirds World is with their identity.

The instruments of decision-making are being worked out against the background of these four factors.

The discussion on instruments of authority

The Archbishop of Canterbury set out the question in his keynote address: 'The problem that confronts us as Anglicans arises not from conflict over the ordination of women, as from the relationship of independent provinces with each other. Although we have machinery for dealing with problems within a diocese and within a province, we have few for those which exist within the communion as a whole.' His question, 'Do we want the Anglican Communion? And if we do, what are we going to do about it?' put the subject of instruments of decision-making on the agenda.

The issue of instruments of decision-making was introduced by Archbishop Keith Rayner from Adelaide. It came as the last part of his paper on authority, which we have already noted in the discussion of reception in Chapter 8. He identified that the question was by what process a communion of autonomous churches, such as the Anglican Communion, could come to a common mind and give authoritative expression to it?

Rediscovering forms of authority

He pointed out that the Anglican Communion and its organs of authority are still evolving. After the Reformation juridical authority was exercised in the Church of England by the Crown and Parliament, but now that authority lies squarely within each Church of the communion. There has been a rediscovery of forms of authority which, while always inherent in the life of the Church, were often submerged. There is a pastoral authority inherent in the episcopate and the ordained ministry, which is exercised both individually and collegially. It involves teaching and nurture through word and sacrament, and its purpose is to preserve the unity of the Church in truth. The authority of the laity has been rediscovered. In synods, at diocesan and provincial (or national) level, bishops, clergy and laity all share in the exercise of authority in the Church.

Resistance to centralization

Archbishop Rayner noted that the Anglican Communion has thus far resisted every proposal for a synod possessing legislative and juridical power over the whole communion, just as it has resisted developing the office of Archbishop of Canterbury into a pan-Anglican primacy. The Lambeth Conference and the Anglican Consultative Council remained obstinately consultative, and the Archbishop of Canterbury remained a focus of our communion and a much-respected first among equals. So there is no office or organ of the whole communion empowered to require conformity to some uniform Anglican stance.

The strength of such a position was that it encouraged the exercise of authority based not on external office and power, but on truth, love and mutual consideration. It was characterized by grace rather than law, by persuasion rather than compulsion—in short, an authority such as that demonstrated by Christ himself.

Its weaknesses were that it was not easy for the Anglican Communion to come quickly to a common mind on controversial matters, and it was too easy for autonomous churches to insist on their legal right to adopt a course that might threaten the integrity and unity of the communion.

He continued to say that the consultative rather than the jurisdictional mode avoided powerful temptations and dangers which accompany the centralization of authority in one office or organ of the Church. But to work effectively, Anglicans needed to develop greater respect for the decisions of synods and the teaching office of bishops and clergy; alongside this respect, a readiness to test searchingly such decisions and teaching in the light of Scripture, tradition and reason; and a willingness to submit local decisions to the judgement of the communion of churches through the consultative process. Anglicans have been too willing at one and the same time to dismiss decisions of properly constituted organs of authority in the Church, and to do so without adequately testing them by the elements of authority which God has given to us.

The international consultative organs—the Lambeth Conference and the Anglican Consultative Council—had an important place in the process. The ACC had two advantages, its frequency of meeting and its inclusion of lay women and men and members of the clergy beside bishops. Yet the Lambeth Conference, in enabling every diocese to have direct representation through its bishop, carried a weight in the communion such as the ACC did not enjoy and, despite the logistical problems, continued to be the most effective consultative organ the communion possessed.

Archbishop Robert Eames, the primate of all-Ireland, made a presentation entitled 'Instruments of Communion and Decision-making: the Development of the Consultative Process in the Anglican Communion'. He identified that the main issue was that 'given our understanding of the Catholic Church not in terms of a centralised institution but as Koinonia, a communion of Churches, what is needed to strengthen the process of Consultation? What is needed to give clearer recognition to the truth that some limitation may be necessary to the discretion of dispersed authority?'

Views from the ACC

How did leaders who had the responsibility of adminstering one of the consultative bodies, the ACC, view the question of authority and decision-making?

The secretary-general, Canon Samuel Van Culin, expressed these views: 'We are at a point in the Anglican Communion where we are catching up with what is happening to us. We are having to discover what responsible inter-Anglican activity in a changing world requires. It requires concentration, a shared publishing, the development of more effective communication structures; a nuanced balance of primatial, episcopal and lay participation in consultation and decision-making.

'I think the Anglican Communion is today reflecting what I once heard the chairman of Boeing Aircraft say: "My problem at Boeing is that there is so much happening in the design department, in the sales department, in the aero-dynamics department, in the metallurgy department, that we do not know what we know. Things are developing in one department that another department needs to know but the information has not got there yet. So we might spend a lot of time and effort in one department trying to accomplish something that another department has already accomplished. One of our management problems at Boeing is to try and find a way to get the parts working more effectively together." That is precisely where we are in the Anglican Communion.

'At this Lambeth Conference the bishops do not know what the ACC is doing. So there is a tendency at the Lambeth Conference to try and limit the ACC; the ACC being in their minds a budget that is costing money to do things that they have never heard about. On the other hand, at Singapore [in 1977] the ACC expressed the feeling that the Lambeth Conference would not really know what was happening in the communion. There were some negative comments at the Singapore meeting about the Lambeth Conference and there are some negative comments at the Lambeth Conference about the ACC. That means what I think the chairman of Boeing said. We have to find a way to help both see and appreciate the extraordinary importance and value of the other as being parts of a growing whole that help the Anglican Communion to be credible and effective as a communion of churches in the world today.'

The chairman of the ACC, Archdeacon Yong Ping Chung, echoed this concern: 'At the beginning of the Conference there was some negative feeling, that the ACC is coming to dominate, promote itself and get more power, maybe because of lack of communications and a host of ignorance about the ACC. As the Conference goes on, people begin to realize what the ACC is doing in serving. The ACC is born out of the provinces, and at any time the provinces, which are the governing body, say we do not want you any more, then the provinces can say so.'

How did Canon Van Culin see the discussion on decision-making? 'This discussion gives people an opportunity to look at the primates and at the fact that there has to be some kind of a budgeting process if you are going to have activities. There has to be some kind of a secretariat that provides the support system and the services and does some of the planning and enables churches to implement what resolutions are passed.

'"Decision-making" needs unpacking. The constitution and canonical decisions are made by the provinces which are the constitutional bodies. The primates can assist in linking the member churches more effectively, rapidly and immediately in matters of faith and order than any other instrument we have; certainly more effectively, immediately and less expensively than the Lambeth Conference or than the Anglican Consultative Council. We could not have a responsible communion if we do not have an increasingly responsible collegial primacy. In a healthy growing mature communion you do not have a collegial primacy at the expense of also a healthy, growing maturing, consultative body which brings the whole ministry of bishops, clergy and laity together. They work together.

'The title "Instruments of Decision-making" is cumbersome but it does not have authority in it. It puts decision-making in a secondary clause. It talks of instruments of consultation and how they contribute to decision-making in the Anglican Communion. Decision-making is still in the local churches. But the primates can have a great deal of influence in the local church, in their own church, and in the process of decision-making. Therefore a collegial primacy with the Archbishop of Canterbury as it matures, develops, and understands itself can be very helpful in effecting more collegial decision-making in the local churches.

'The ACC is just a consultative body but, as such, is essential to an international household of churches that operate and live in different cultures, under different languages and in different synodical systems. Consultation becomes essential to them. What the ACC does is build networks for shared work; sustain and implement the dialogues. Look how many resolutions tabled at the Conference are asking the ACC to develop a more effective inter-Anglican communication system; to undertake new ecumencial dialogues. That is appropriate. It has not yet been reflected in the structural resolutions. That will come.'

Commenting after the Conference, the vice-chairman of the ACC, Canon Colin Craston from England, said: 'Care must be taken to ensure the consultative role with laity and clergy in the

ACC does not suffer an imbalance—though neither Lambeth nor the ACC itself desires a formal Synod for the Communion. With the two-fold expression of authority here outlined there is always the possibility of bishops emphasizing their own distinctive role in authority, if feeling impatient with synodical processes. It is the very natural reaction—"Leave it to us!" Something of this was evident at Lambeth. Indeed, theological and other consultants, and ACC laity and clergy, experienced frustration along these lines. And it has to be said that while the bishop's responsibility includes guardianship of the faith, not all bishops by any means are theologically equipped for the task. The consultative exercise, and adequate theological resources, are both essential to responsible episcopacy.'

Views of the Archbishop of Canterbury

The Archbishop of Canterbury expressed in the debate his welcome for an enhanced role for the Primates' Meeting: 'We have experienced its value and this resolution recognizes the accepted and acceptable authority it possesses. As with all inter-Anglican agencies, its authority is moral rather than legislative. But the primates are those entrusted with the leadership of the Churches and are thus recognizably representative of the whole Communion. For swift and effective action, whether on doctrinal questions or for concentrated support in time of crisis you need easy communication.

'If, however, we enhance the role of the Primates' Meeting we must expect it to affect the role and work of the Anglican Consultative Council. Although the ACC has representation from the Provinces, its claim to be representative is more modest. People are chosen for it in varying ways, and not necessarily because they carry leadership in their churches. This is not to dismiss its value. As a Communion, we owe much to the ACC in enhancing our inter-dependence and increasing our mutual trust. But I think we might be further strengthened if it was explicitly recognized that members of the ACC should be selected from the Provinces on the basis of their specialist skills and knowledge, and perhaps the ability to represent special interest groups, thus complementing, even serving, the Primates' Meeting, in its increased responsibilities. Whether or not this proves to be the way forward, we must do more thinking about the relationship between the ACC and the Primates.

'The Anglican Communion has always resisted the idea of a Pan Anglican Synod. I think we have been wise to do so. If we are to be a Communion which recognizes its need for strengthening its inter-dependence, I am sure the effective way of doing it is through the Primates' Meetings. Giving an enhanced role for the Archbishop of Canterbury or creating a central synod—these are dangerous avenues. They are attempts to structure ourselves over against other Communions. We must not lose our character as a provisional Communion—always seeking a wider unity than our own. We should not be ashamed that such untidiness or informality has enabled us to move into United Churches whether in the Indian Sub-Continent or in China.

'Secondly a word about the appointment of the Archbishop of Canterbury. . . . We should cherish our roots but keep the Archbishop of Canterbury cut down to size as essentially a diocesan bishop, and not a constitutional monarch or alternative Pope.'

The official press release of the Conference identified the significance of these decisions. The enhanced responsibility of the Primates 'could curtail the authority of the Archbishop of Canterbury, and, ironically, of the Lambeth Conference itself. The resolution also adds a new element to these four traditional instruments of Anglican authority and unity. It calls for regional conferences to take place between Lambeths. The ultimate effect of such meetings in the decision-making process is unknown.' These regional meetings were a contribution from the Two Thirds World.

Two Thirds World perspectives:

Regional meetings

A new element of regional meetings appeared to emerge out of the concerns of the African and Asian regional groups. The bishops from those areas evidenced a strong concern to have such regional meetings. The Africa region clearly set a trend in its pre-Lambeth meeting at Limuru, Kenya, in 1987, its meeting in Cambridge just prior to Lambeth, its plenary at the Conference, and the continued regional meetings at the Conference. Archbishop Browne described the regional meetings in this way: 'The Africa regional meetings were very important because strangely enough, the very first time the Africa region met as a region was last year when we were considering Lambeth themes. We had 50 per cent of the bishops from Africa and all but one of the provinces were represented. That was the first time we ever got together across the continent to discuss the issues of the Church. That was a foretaste of what Lambeth would be. That is why we kept calling the regional meeting back, saying, "Let's hear what you say about this or that issue." One of the helpful things about the regional meeting was that at those meetings we were going to review those resolutions prior to their coming up on the plenary floor.'

Bishops from Latin America had recently come from the first Continental Anglican congress. Onell Soto remembered it as 'very lively; there was singing and dancing and making jokes and playing the guitar. Here at Lambeth we feel restrained, we cannot do that. Here we have to behave better. There it was more informal; it was a camp and we could wear shorts. It was not a fancy conference, this was very fancy. In a room the size of my single room here in Lambeth there were four people in bunk-beds, two bishops and two priests. In order to climb into my bed I had to step on the other guy and we had only one shower. It was more Third World, more in accord with the reality with which we live.

'We discussed and argued. One of the values was the possibility of people coming from the southern cone, and the people in the north of Latin America in the ninth province of the Episcopal Church of the United States of America—including Mexico, Central America, and Panama. It was valuable for people from the ninth province to see that Anglicans can talk about a faith and say "I was converted, I can speak of my personal faith and witness to that." That was a very healthy exchange without any big arguments.

'One of the decisions we have taken here at Lambeth is that all the bishops would meet in 1990 in Brazil which is celebrating its centenary then. We hope to invite African and Asian bishops too. When I see Africa and Asia I see that we have many issues in common. It is a challenge to me to see this. So this Lambeth Conference has been a sort of second stage, midway between our two regional gatherings.'

Decision-making by consensus

Archbishop Browne told us of the African way of decision-making by consensus: 'Africans normally arrive at decisions by consensus. The dimension that that adds to episcopacy is that making a decision simply because you are at the top, or making a decision because 51 per cent of the number, a simple majority, approves of that. It is important to have some further consultation even after a simple majority vote. That aspect of the African traditional way of making decisions we bring to episcopacy. When we made our presentation on the issue of the ordination of women, because it is of such a divisive nature, we reported that we are calling for a consensus on a provincial level before a move of that type is made, not just for a simple majority. This process of consensus is not quite like the one party system in our governments because that system does not allow for other views at all. We listen to the group that dissents because African philosophy says, "I am because we are, I do not exist distinct from the corporate body. Even if I dissent I am still part of the body and I want to maintain the unity of the body." In Liberia, we were originally linked with the American Episcopal Church, and from that background we had a more democratic process. We had women on the Standing Committee and in the ministry. So the bishop was not just president of the synod, he was one of the group. That kind of democracy brought over from America has brought a lot more democratization of the Church than other Churches had.'

Archbishop Browne gave an example of how the African decision-making procedure helped them at their meetings: 'We dealt with the polygamy situation in the following way. I was going to speak clearly against the polygamy motion. But after we got into our regional meeting, Archbishop Kuria, even though presiding at the meeting, told us that the Province of Kenya's constitution was in line with that resolution. Once he said that, and Archbishop Makhulu from Central Meeting had said that he was in favour of the motion, we knew very well that we would be running an uphill battle, fighting against the African consensus. I said that if this issue comes up I will fight against it. But the Province of Kenya said that they were already doing it. We regarded that move of the province as delaying tactics; that the province has accepted it in theory but done nothing about it. So the effect of the Lambeth motion is to give a push. With that kind of explanation, the consensus came.'

Bishop Michael Nazir-Ali holds that: 'the resolution on instruments of communion is very significant for the future of the communion. The Conference gave an enhanced role to the primates in the process of inter-Anglican consultation. This is a move away from a more quasi-synodical structure. The role of the ACC was clearly restricted to its present position.'

Bishop Nazir-Ali points out further that: 'the Lambeth Conference, the Anglican Consultative Council and the Primates' Meeting are not Anglican bodies *simpliciter*, they are now bodies where bishops from a broad cross-section in communion with each other take counsel together. This is an embodiment of a proper theology of communion. It pushes beyond the United Churches of South Asia to the Old Catholics, the Mar Thoma and the Philippines Independent Churches, which are all churches with whom the Anglican Communion is in communion and needs to push beyond that. This inclusion of bishops from churches where Anglicans have united with Christians of other traditions underlines the seriousness with which Anglicanism takes its provisionality. Anglicanism is willing to be transformed in the interests of Christian unity into a more inclusive family of churches. If this is the case theologically, it must become the case ecclesiologically. The structures of the Anglican Communion must begin to reflect this.'

The primate of West Africa, Archbishop George Browne, thought that the resolutions on instruments of communion would be of great significance and importance. He told us: 'When the primates met together a few years ago, we asked ourselves, what is it that keeps the communion together. Certainly it is no longer the creeds. It is no longer the English language that used to keep the communion together, it is no longer the prayer book. That is why we asked for us to take a hard look at the structure at this Conference. If that commission comes out with a good report, I am looking forward to that being one of the issues for the next Lambeth.

'They did send out the book on *Authority in the Anglican Communion*[1] about a year ago—but, as is typical, not all of us understood it. Now that you have more than one bishop from an area going back, we really hope we can take Lambeth with us to the dioceses and that will be one way. I intend to take not only these resolutions, but the resolutions about the structures and ask my chancellor to take a look at it and make some suggestions so that our next synod can react to it on the basis of the resolution. Because I can foresee this whole subject of the structure being an ongoing subject.'

The role of the Archbishop of Canterbury

The Conference did not become a Conference of personalities or of stars. The Archbishop of Canterbury had such a clear run because he was the only personality. And even he, by deliberately allowing the other primates to take the chair, by underplaying his own role very much, encouraged their role to develop and therefore enhanced himself. He became a corporate personality within the primates because he pushed others forward. The best close-up picture of the Anglican Communion at the Conference was at the end of his closing address, when all the primates came up to join him at the podium to shake his hand and embrace him. The Archbishop affirmed them by sharing his role with them and developing a sense of collegiality throughout the Conference.

The Two Thirds World bishops were quite concerned to give the Archbishop of Canterbury an important role. Yet their concern was much more a personal affirmation of Robert Runcie and his own role, rather than a desire to perpetuate Canterbury-centricity. English bishops affirmed how important Canterbury was as owned by England. England does not want to lose its Canterbury. There was a strong plea from the floor to take your hands off our Archbishop. But the English bishops may have misunderstood the concerns of the Two Thirds World bishops. The Two Thirds World bishops were saying we really want Robert Runcie. It is not certain that they really wanted Canterbury. For one thing they would not have the money to repair the cathedral.

Their affirmation of Robert Runcie was not a desire to take over the see of Canterbury—they were more likely saying 'The Church and nation of England do not really want your Archbishop—look at the way your press treats him. We want your Archbishop—do not think we want your Canterbury.' They are prepared for Canterbury, provided it is seen as a place for both Britain as well as the focus of the Anglican Communion. The Canterbury-centredness that seemed to be coming in is probably not a deep commitment and will probably disappear. They did not want an Anglican Pope at Canterbury. But they did want a focus of unity and decided that that should be the Primates' Meeting.

Resolution on decision-making

The resolution passed by the Conference read as follows:
'This Conference:

2.(a) Urges that encouragement be given to a developing collegial role for the Primates' Meeting under the presidency of the Archbishop of Canterbury, so that the Primates' Meeting is able to exercise an enhanced responsibility in offering guidance on doctrinal, moral and pastoral matters.

2.(b) Recommends that in the appointment of any future Archbishop of Canterbury, the Crown Appointments Commission be asked to bring the Primates of the Communion into the process of consultation.

3. Resolves that the Lambeth Conference as a conference of bishops of the Anglican Communion should continue in future, at appropriate intervals.

4. Recommends that Regional Conferences of the Anglican Communion should meet between Lambeth Conferences as and when the Region concerned believes it to be appropriate; and in the event of these Regional Conferences being called, it should be open to the region concerned to make them representative of clergy and laity as well as bishops.

5. Recommends that the ACC continue to function as a coordinating agency within the Anglican Communion; and that it should do so in close co-operation with the Primates' Meeting.'

An explanation to the resolution stated: 'We see an enhanced role for the Primates as a key to a growth of inter-dependence within the Communion. We do not see any inter-Anglican jurisdiction as possible or desirable; an inter-Anglican synodical structure would be virtually unworkable and highly expensive. A collegial role for the Primates, by contrast, could easily be developed, and their collective judgement and advice would carry considerable weight.'

What is communion?

What are the limits of communion and of comprehensiveness? Is it automatic now that some of these people are no longer in communion? Can the communion contain people who do not recognize each other at all? How can churches that do not recognize one another be in the same communion? Should there be a way in which people can help each other to live together? In a real sense, this underlying issue of the instruments of communion was ducked. It was handed over to a commission to look after. On the issue of the nature of communion, the bishops took away from Lambeth as many questions as answers.

Notes

1. Stephen Sykes, ed., *Authority in the Anglican Communion* (Toronto, Anglican Book Centre, 1987).

CHAPTER 10

Taking Lambeth with Them

What were the Lambeth bishops going back to? As the double-decker buses loaded with bishops and their wives and luggage were pulling out of the forecourt of Eliot College on the campus of the University of Kent at the end of the Conference, a North American bishop shouted from the steps of the college to his friends on the bus: 'Enjoy your honeymoon!' It was not to be a honeymoon for the Burmese bishops who returned to a revolution. In Kenya, Bishop Gitari returned to attacks on television by the President against his reported views on polygamy. In South Africa, Desmond Tutu soon courted arrest in advising people not to vote in the October 1988 elections.

What were they taking with them?

First, they took with them a sense of what the communion was all about. Roger Herfft felt, 'A greater sense of belonging to a world-wide family that is far greater than the "English" Church.' Maurice Goodall from Christchurch, New Zealand, would leave with 'a strength of fellowship based on Bible Study and prayer—a key for our clergy and laity for the future.' For David Evans from Peru, 'belonging to a family of churches that has a historical continuity is a source of strength. I believe a federation rather than a communion better describes our reality. I do not think I really believe in "full", "half", or "impaired" communion.' A bishop from South Africa commented, 'It was the sheer openness and affection, a sudden and then growing realization that we belonged to a communion that was immensely worthwhile—a sense that the Anglican Communion matters and that it helps in some situations to give the identity of a world context to some Third World provinces that badly need it.' Another spoke of leaving with 'hope for the future of the Anglican Communion. God is using this great family'.

The Bishop of Seoul took a new perspective on servant leadership. He was having a meal with the Archbishop of Canterbury, who got up to fetch their coffee. It struck him that if this person to whom he gave great respect could be the waiter with coffee, then that is how he himself should serve his colleagues at home. In a society where much emphasis is placed on respect, that made a great impact.

All the bishops from the Western world who responded to us, spoke of the impact made on their lives by the bishops from the Two Thirds World. Bishop David Sheppard of Liverpool, England, was impressed by one bishop who told how he had learnt that he was number one on the list for removal by the political authorities; though he heard that the numbers two and three on the list had already been removed, he had refused the opportunity to go on a particular conference and stayed at home instead. Bishop Sheppard was impressed by the strong awareness of the presence of these bishops, of their struggles to relate the gospel to their cultures, and to the huge pressures of poverty, starvation, refugees and war. He will take to his diocese 'a firm attempt to spread the awareness of belonging to one church in God's one world'; others spoke of taking back 'the reality of their faith in more difficult circumstances than most of us meet'; 'their vitality and concern for evangelism'; 'an inspiration and a rebuke to us all'.

The Two Thirds World bishops took with them the strong sense that they related as equals: able to hold their own, make an impact and be respected. And Lambeth had made its own impact on them. One Nigerian bishop on his return from Lambeth was greeted with a brand new Mercedes-Benz car at the airport. Such a gift is a traditional honour for a leader returning from an important visit abroad in recognition of his achievement. But Lambeth had so changed this bishop that he refused even to look at it, and ordered that it be disposed of before he entered the diocese.

What was the contribution of these bishops to Lambeth? For Maurice Goodall, 'Lambeth was much better than expected because of the developing world's contribution. To see the primates together makes us Western Europeans realize that the centre of gravity has changed. Were 9 out of the 27 primates Europeans?' These bishops also made a significant contribution 'in small groups, in the increasing concern shown by attendance at revival meetings on the last three mornings at 6 a.m. and through the impact of the African and Pacific presentations'. Compared to 1978, Spanish and French was used for the first time in plenary sessions, and there were far greater contributions from the Two Thirds World bishops. For one bishop, it was 'good to have the Lambeth fathers discussing a non-Western subject like polygamy'. The Two Thirds World bishops contributed 'the reality of courageous witness under persecution, of spontaneous growth through evangelism, and the simplicity and directness of their faith'.

The stories also impressed the bishops: 'A bishop in our group was forced to live apart from his wife and children because of the great dangers. He had his home burnt down twice. We shared his pain and suffering in our group'; stories of evangelism in Ecuador, witness in Pakistan, persecution in Nigeria, Uganda and the Sudan, growth of the Church under persecution in Mozambique, such that the old church buildings were inadequate when they were reopened legally; and the huge size of many African dioceses where, for example, one Ugandan diocese has 940 congregations.

Not all the bishops were completely happy with the African contributions. While some saw the African bishops as welcome champions of orthodoxy, others perceived them as the avoiders of questions and sought to marginalize their contribution in subtle ways.

For example, it was suggested that in one case that they did not understand the point at issue. The Africans strongly resisted the attempt by Bishop Moore of New York to bring in a resolution affirming the human rights of homosexuals. Some North Americans argued that the resistance of the Africans was based on a misunderstanding of the motion as one that condoned homosexuality. Manasses Kuria strongly opposes this interpretation of their resistance: 'We acknowledge that homosexuals have rights as human beings, but they do not have rights as homosexuals. Homosexuality is sin. We do not call homosexuals to be faithful in marriage to one another. That is to call sin holy.'

Two further responses emerged in the press conference after the debate. First, the African response was called emotional. Yet, in a press conference before the session, Bishop Moore noted that he had personal experience of the issue of homosexuality, as both his uncle (who had visited their family regularly) and one of his own sons were homosexual. One wonders whose emotions were more deeply involved. A second response was that when the Africans became more developed societies and faced the same pressures of urbanization and secularization they would change their views. This of course begs the question as to which society would develop in which direction. The Archbishop of the West Indies was very clear in personal conversation that he for one had no desire for his society to develop in the same way as the United States.

A fourth response to African culture was voiced by the Archbishop of York, John Habgood, in the last of the programmes entitled 'The Lambeth Walk' on Channel 4. He indicated that the growth of the Church in Africa was due to the fact that the African people were responding to a faith more in tune with modern scientific culture than their primitive culture had been. Desmond Tutu could not let that remark pass by unchallenged. He pointed out that in many cases the African culture was more in harmony with the biblical world view than Western culture was. John Habgood's only reply was to indicate that this was typical of the exchanges that had taken place throughout Lambeth. We wondered if the African bishops were continually having to correct such views from other Western bishops.

Taking Lambeth to the dioceses

Archbishop George Browne of Liberia told us: 'We brought our dioceses hopefully to Lambeth. Now we have got to take Lambeth to the dioceses. For myself, this means going through the resolutions, digesting them, putting them to my synod for reflection and discussion, getting my synod's view and then when it is time for provincial synod, going to the provincial synod and saying "coming out of Lambeth, this resolution my diocese has discussed and this is the diocesan view". Hopefully if other bishops do the same, then that is bringing Lambeth to the provinces.'

He told us that one of the things he would take with him would be insights. Friendships have to be nurtured over a period. He would not see some of these people for the next ten years and, like many of them, would not have the time to do personal correspondence. But he would take the penetrating insights that he had gained from the Bible Studies. Even though there were guidelines in the Bible Studies, they brought personal viewpoints into the studies and discussion. If in it he was stupid or ignorant, the other members had no hesitation in exposing it. It is this insight that he would take back. When he had his next clergy conference he hoped to conduct Bible Studies along those lines—to say 'How do you read this? Let us see how it affects your own life.'

He said: 'I have been able to appreciate at a deeper level what is taking place in other parts of the world. At first I was more preoccupied with Africa, and West Africa in particular. Now, hearing the people from the Pacific, the Sudan, and from Ireland has given me a deeper insight and appreciation so that when I hear on the news that this thing is happening in so and so place it means more to me now than a month ago.'

Continuing in communion

If one feeling dominated the ending of the 1988 Lambeth Conference, it was a tremendous desire to remain in communion together. Even Graham Leonard, the Bishop of London, who came nearest to sounding as though he would leave, eventually pulled back.

Why do these bishops want to stay together? Is it because they are so outnumbered and under pressure that unless they stay together they will be easy targets for being picked off and thus sink individually? As we were writing this final section the news came through that Barbara Harris had been consecrated as the first woman bishop in the Anglican Communion, within six months of the end of the Conference. And thus far the communion is still in one piece. Perhaps it is fundamental to Anglicanism not to want to make final, irrevocable judgements in haste; to be willing to shelve matters for a while and get on with the things that can unite rather than concentrate on what divides. Certainly, the Bible Studies around the word of God was a gloriously uniting experience.

Any talk of instruments of communion must take this reality into consideration. The experience of the Bible Studies was not a matter of sharing exegetical analysis and insights alone; bishops shared their stories of mission in context as bishops around the word of God in a setting of prayer and worship. This was partnership in mission come alive. True partnership in mission is not so much a programme as a way of life, as people share their stories of mission. The cement that held the communion together at the Conference came not through instruments of decision-making, but through hearing stories of mission around the word of God. This is the creative source of the bonds of affection.

The communion will stay together through working jointly on mission, ministry and sharing round the word, not through perfect instruments of communion. This feeling of togetherness cannot be taken for granted. Creative ways must be found of encouraging it. The present instruments on their own will not be adequate to do this. The continent-wide meetings were especially valued in the pre-Lambeth preparation and at Lambeth itself. They will be important instruments of communion. In the Two Thirds World great importance is given to the Partners in Mission process. A Canadian bishop whom we met at a Partners in Mission consultation in Kenya, declared himself surprised and rebuked by the enormous investment and importance placed on Partners in Mission by the Province of Kenya—which put his own province to shame.

In the ecumenical context the mission and ministry statements of the WCC and of the Lausanne Movement are powerful instruments for keeping movements together and united. If the Anglican Church is to be seen as a movement, a provisional grouping of churches seeking the unity to which all Christians are called, then the most significant contribution to keeping the communion together may be the Common Declaration that was prepared. The Lambeth Quadrilateral gives the basis of communion as common adherence to Scripture, to the historic creeds as articulating the mind of Scripture, the celebration of the dominical sacraments of baptism and holy communion, and maintenance of the apostolic ministry. Bishop Michael Nazir-Ali holds that, 'what Anglicans say about relations with other Christians is equally true about Anglicans themselves. This is the basis both of our communion together and on which we hope to build our relations with other churches. If we abandon that, then we have a family, a common ethos, affection, a federation of churches but not a communion.'

It was here that Bishop Nazir-Ali felt that the United Churches make such a contribution to the Lambeth Conference and the Anglican Communion. For they could say with a certain amount of coherence (which others do not) that the Lambeth Quadrilateral is the basis both of their own communion internally and of their communion with the Anglican Communion and not any historical accidents, the Empire, the Anglican system, fellow feeling or bonds of affection—which could all be very vague and insubstantial.

Bishop Nazir-Ali continued: 'The catholicity of the Anglican Communion is tested by its communion with the Mar Thoma, the Old Catholics, the United Churches and the Philippines Independent Catholic Church, because here they all come from different traditions, and communion together has to be based on a common recognition of faith and not on fellow feeling or the old school tie.'

Thus any continuation of communion has to be based on lasting theological foundations rather than on relying on historical accidents to evoke feelings of brotherhood and to keep the communion together. The participation of the United Churches from South Asia and from China was an important sign of that basis. It is very sad that the Anglican Churches in Canada, Nigeria and East Africa failed to carry through their church union schemes for narrow parochial reasons. Such union is not without risk. The Church of South India was prepared to risk non-attendance at the Lambeth Conference for the sake of Church unity and did not come for forty years. They were prepared to risk not Christ, but their traditions, for the sake of communion. Communion requires risk. That risk has become less, but will still exist.

Partnership through sharing round the word of God with stories of mission; a common declaration in a theological basis for communion; and willingness to risk not Christ but the Church for the sake of communion: these may be the most powerful instruments for facilitating the unity that, as the experience of the 1988 Lambeth Conference convinced everyone who attended it, was a precious and divine gift in a fractured and divided world.